1987

SAVAGE COMEDY SINCE KING UBU:

A Tangent To "The Absurd"

By
Kenneth Steele White

University Press
of America™

Contents

1

Since Alfred Jarry's <u>King Ubu</u> (1896), savage comedy in Western Europe and the United States has been radical, more in degree than in outlook. Its ferocious satire and honed-edge, sharp bite had been known in theater at least since the time of Aristophanes.

One perplexing and celebrated instance had been Shakespeare's play, <u>Troilus and Cressida</u> (1609). Scathing, darkly comic, iconoclastic, far-sighted, the comedy insinuates affinities of lust and war-making. Shakespeare's hyperboles of pre-willed and strange human ineptness sharpen futility. <u>Troilus and Cressida</u> taps acrid theater's virulent springs.

More complex were certain new, ironic goads. Thersites' viperish, unbelieving tongue could belong to the twentieth century. Love and non-love in conjunction flood with the ambivalences we may identify as ours today. And Ulysses' view of cosmic misalignment is prophetic of recent plays.

Colored by King Ubu's nightmarish ludicrousness, French comedy between 1896 and 1975 remodeled derisory viewpoints. War, the machine, social upheavals, threats posed by science and exacerbated hopes for a new day and individual freedom brought with them tensions, singly or in combinations. Fresh types of theater began to burgeon. Some contained unheard-of omens, or harbingers.

What was "savage comedy"? It was disenchanted, quizzical. Laughter dredged up fear. One "certainty" it toppled was the long-held claim that a dramatic character must evolve, accumulating more facets in depth as he progresses.

Savage comedy broke through many of the frontiers that had separated comic and tragic. In its derisiveness, it incarnated fears that human nature was wrapped in coils, held in the processes of metamorphosis. In Ionesco's <u>Rhinoceros</u> (1959), when ordinary men and women agree to become four-footed, stampeding pachyderms and to join the herd, this metaphor reached new artistic truths.

Implied or enacted, imagistically puzzling, transformations in species and kind gained momentum during the decades from 1896 to 1975. Latent metamorphoses appeared and reappeared. Changes in form crystallized without warning. As in a delirium-erected prism, dream-like generic jumps multiplied.

Backlash typified intransigeant rebels. Their ripostes were intended to unloosen life's pincers: indoctrination, self-pretense that shrivels the pretender, aging, tedium, science's stranglehold on human survival. At the base of this revolt was a shudder of recognition. The horror of the modern self was intimated, as it careened toward a bottomless whirlpool, destination nothingness.

To combat the shackles of moral paralysis, was savage-comic laughter enough? Could it provide a derisory catharsis? During some (though not all) performances of savage comedies, moments of hilarity (and many more of inner laughter) crept in. Restlessly. The spectator, ill at ease when faced with shadows of his own futilities, tended to be either mystified or indignant. Worst of all, he could no longer feel assured that his reactions had validity. His psyche, assembling feelings on inhabitual surfaces, ran into trouble. It refused to adapt when plunged into slippery dramatic craftiness, which touched on rapacity's comic trigger.

ONE: SAVAGE COMEDY (JARRY'S KING UBU TO DURRENMATT AND ALBEE)

Has the Cosmos been wrenched out of its natural tracks; is it awry, queasy? If, since Shakespeare, dramatists have put forth similarly disabused questions, what theatrical overturnings have crystallized? Has a twentieth-century queasiness led to foreshadowings of change, future evolutions?

The precocious French playwright, Alfred Jarry, gave grotesque shape in King Ubu (1896) to a covert, ever-growing suspicion that a fault was cleaving the Cosmos. King Ubu, hyperbole disguised as farce, extends an animalistic metaphor of man's rapacity, perhaps even of his future. Ubu's semi-ludicrous ferocity eats away the bases of logic. One embodiment of beastly imagery comes and goes so quickly that we are inclined to overlook it. An immense, voracious wild bear mirrors Ubu's ambitions (usurping the throne, mass killings, gleeful revenge). The animal outlines secrets of Ubu's devouring conscience. Craven, the usurper-King flees. He lets fellow-conspirators kill the bear. Through metaphor, our consciousness of evil seems to be swallowed, obliterated. Ubu, in misshapen and wild imagery, points to something modern: the possibility of series of metamorphoses spurred by voracity's genetics, key to man's tomorrows, to his yet unknown being.

Just before the end of their macabre adventures, King Ubu and cohorts, turning their backs on wanton slaughters, now without clear destinations, are adrift on the sea. They have no roots, no home, almost no reason for existence. Their small ship's aimlessness figuratively signals the vagabonds' refusal to conceive of their lives as rational or necessary. Without saying so explicitly, they spurn acceptance of the earth's logic. Jarry forces us to envision an extravagant universe as ungovernable as an ocean tossing out of control. In King Ubu's idiotic wars in nowhere-land, there is no guiding azimuth for humanity on earth or at sea.

Shudders of barbarism had already tinted nineteenth-century French poetry and novels. One vein was a semi-chimerical literary dream: to sabotage society's thought patterns by concocting "verbal alchemy." This alchemic wizardry would sap underpinnings and pillars of conservatism. France's outstanding poets of the times, from Hugo to Nerval, Lautréamont, Baudelaire and Rimbaud, all strove toward some kind of alchemic formulae, each author in his own way. Combined, their influences were vast. Few made society wobble.

In novel and short story, the phenomenon was curious. Flaubert's scenes of barbaric ecstasy in Salammbô (1862) or Hérodias (1877), Merimée's quiver of "fittingness" in the grisly father-son murder of Matéo Falcone (1829), and, toward century's end, Huysman's Mephistophelian reversals of life-balance (A Rebours, 1884) are memorable.

After 1896, avant-garde drama in France and Western Europe intimated new revelations of rifts in cosmic stability. A quasi-Hamletic anxiety intensified. The universe's orbit was deemed imperfect, impermanent. Changing theories recast beliefs in the physics and the astronomy of the universe. Theater's ideological presuppositions melted. Questioned skeptically were age-old concepts that the Cosmos was an ideal model for man's choices of how and where to find the secret of the self on earth. Issues of comparable scope were rife.

Savage comedy's roots are ancient. Release of frenzied or subconsciously repressed instincts through artistic reinvention is ageless. Lascaux's prehistoric cave drawings reflect the hunter's terrors and almost as surely, his sexual exorcisms. Comedy's twisting ironies, derisory shapes and misconnections at times hint fearful awe at Nature's battles among social levels and antagonistic species.

Dionysiac fervor (as well as other ancient Greek, ritualized revelries), with rhythm's feverishness at apogee racing toward the brink of riotousness, mime and dance orchestrating the elements' powers, showed perils of psychic libertinisms which French authors, like others in Europe and America, were to imply, even to dramatize, on stage. These constituted figurative omens. Eerie implications emerged. Genet and Arrabal insinuated sex transfers, Albee genetic tyranny, Anouilh life as fragmented nightmare, and Jarry and Dürrenmatt the intellect's warfare as hyperbole for the small combats that make up existence. The master, Pirandello, was to outline the soul's shadows doubling and redoubling: the untouchable substance which is in fact life's fiber.

Interspersed are subtler stage transmutations, provided by dramatists as different as Strindberg, Anouilh, Beckett, Pinter, Tchekhov, and Tennessee Williams, among others.

Savage comedy, not a rigid, tight concept, is supple. Its outer boundaries are enlargeable. They stretch, to some degree, to fill voids as tragedy disappears. Bizarre, surrealistic exuberance has helped to color many savage plays. Others are secretive, compressing in inward-directed coils: Samuel Beckett's back-toward-the-womb scenic parables curl through introspections. However masked, elements in common can be glimpsed.

In a few caustic comedies, a neo-Dionysiac image resurges: frenzies of life and death as parallelisms. During ecstasies produced by Dionysiac revels, life-giving and death-dealing instincts twinned. Mortal excess, in celebration, fringed death's territories.

A propos is one modern analogy. During the 1930's, marathon dancers in the United States, goaded by Depression miseries, underwent outlandish, physically tortured "festivity" to prove stamina and life-will. Some died in the process.

The cause of such deaths, an ageless paradox, reaffirms quizzical alliances of life-force and death-wish. In marathon dancing, the motive was money. Less visible, other stimuli lurked. Unwary or complusive marathoners, in fact, may have

6

danced compulsively to defy or to lure death. By intuition, they plunged past mortal limits. Two ecstasies--daring to tempt mortality and finding the bodily perils of festiveness--emerged, sometimes fused.

The Springtime excitement incarnated by Dionysus, symbol of Nature's rebirth and transformations, reappears in astonishing guises. Savage comedy is infused with erotic awakenings, virility and fecundity, passion for life and its promise of longevity.

What has been wrongly viewed as misanthropy or scorn for life (King Ubu, a majority of Anouilh's wry plays, parts of Arrabal's and Beckett's theater) is in reality almost the opposite. It is disguised yearning-to-keep-life-meaningfully-going. It is a springboard which launches glimmers of hope in many savage plays.

The function of unworldliness in savage comedy is debatable. Ubu's gyrations, kinetic though burlesque, his parodies of war, his mechanical exterminations of enemies, his ship-on-nowhere-ocean are cases in point: as metaphors of modern dread, each carves a theatrical trail. Each conveys effects akin to those created by superlative mime and dance. One key feature of ancient dance was that, at zeniths, it transmitted what Nature was in stages of becoming.

Rain dances in modern times, adapted from early prototypes, copy the divining aims of ritual. From divination to prophecy is but a step. It is no coincidence that savage comedy exudes implied forebodings.

Ritual fetes in ancient Greece and Rome often had sacred dimensions. Celebrants linked worship of forces in Nature with new mental life, creativity. Some stance toward sacredness, not always absolute among the ancients, is occasionally crucial in savage comedies. Twentieth-century playwrights rather seldom venerate the old gods, Christian or pagan. (Among the exceptions are Giraudoux and Arrabal.).

7

An outrageous subject of adoration came to the fore: man, flabby and vicious though he may seem to be. After King Ubu, its gleeful mayhem, ferocity, improvised words, and animalistic omens, the growth of French savage comedy accelerated. This expansion took six or seven main paths.

Radical evolutions occurred. "Savage" is at best a rather open-ended term. A number of formulae can help to make it clear. Savage comedy has these distinguishing marks:

I. Ultimate Metaphorical Aims:
   A. To intimate that Cosmos, science and society are flawed, degrading mechanisms.
   B. To convey belief that new types of fierce riposte against these adversaries are imperatives.

II. Thematics:
   A. Reflections of life's queasiness and transitoriness by thematic splintering, frequently unresolved. Hyperbolic ruthlessness as enemy.
   B. The anti-hero's recoil in aversion and revolt. It is a typical world-stance, outlined in atmospheres of caustic, caricatured uneasiness.

III. Figurative Tones:
   A. Individualistically untamed; quasi-brutal or anthropomorphic; ominous, queasy; Cosmic in figurative dreads; barbarous; wavering, as in metamorphoses; prophetic or apocalyptic; oneiric; nightmarishly excessive; torn, unfinished.

IV. Structure:
   A. Multilinearity, fragmentation fused mainly on metaphorical levels; dreamlike or unreal. Uneasiness; "pending" forms.

As W.B. Yeats remarked after having seen a performance of

8

Jarry's <u>King Ubu</u> in 1896, the farce is "half comic, half eerie."[1]
Often described, <u>King Ubu</u>'s other-worldliness and unique nature
are still shrouded. Ubu the bestial usurper, comic-savage center
of Jarry's Cosmos, spurts out a kind of raw, imagistic language
which is his alone, wars without warring in a spurious nowhere,
eats bear that is more than bear, makes massacre ludicrous, and
at last, on high seas, is the ocean's toy in a laughably metaphorical ship, destination almost zero. Jarry himself, offering
an unusual metaphysical hint, pinpointed the paradoxical absolute
he sought (eternity) in all this imprecision and aimlessness:
"the better to suggest eternal things."[2]

Yeats' historical exclamation, just after viewing <u>King Ubu</u>,
"After us the savage God,"[3] has multiplied in the powers of its
prediction. Yeats also gave a prophetic label (Savage) to Jarry
and his buffoonish Ubu.

What species of new Savage God was imminent in Western theater? The half-century that followed King Ubu's animality was to
grow monstrous new deities, some single-headed, others many-
headed. Theater's savages and human hybrids gestated.

The Ubuesque hyperbole—idiotic advancement from bestiality
to obliteration of adversaries—is a strange, new cycle. It
turns and crushes like a giant millwheel. At the same time, it
tilts, askew, ravages those in its way. One realizes that Ubu's
dream as conqueror ("the rapacious will devour the merely voracious") is cracked. In the core of the monster's wild universe
is a chasm.

Since Aristophanes' <u>Lysistrata</u> (a favorite production in
Western theaters while the war in Viet-Nam lasted), one comic-
ironic mythos suggested the body's triumphs over carnage and
death's haste. Ionesco's <u>Macbett</u> (1972) and <u>The King Dies</u> (1962)
underlined this ambiguously "doomed" erotic stamina, as it seems
to delay death's arrival.

A shocking counter-current—love <u>makes</u> war—co-existed. Two
of the most startling instances were Shakespeare's <u>Troilus and</u>

9

Cressida and Giraudoux's Tiger at the Gates (1935). In the Shakespearean satire, Cressida, nearly a sheer aphrodisiac power, helps to provoke war's resumption; Helen exerts even more direct bellicose force in Giraudoux's play.

After King Ubu, savage comedies were skeptical of the body's chances of forestalling decay and death. Hamlet's split shadow lingered. Beside it was Aristophanes' gusty exuberance --whether mask of terror or active libido.

Like Hamlet, doubled and redoubled in contemporaneous implications, savage masterpieces of the twentieth century exposed ribald facets. In King Ubu, the anti-hero as macabre actor of his own burlesque destiny is also a derisive inventor of new slices of human nature. One means is unearthly language. Ubu embodies an anti-ethic. He also hints a mini-Cosmos of inanity, brutality and non-principle. Jarry's barbarism transfigures ribaldry. He makes unworldly gusto turn into grayness almost bereft of purpose.

In Ubu's nowhere-land, thought's savagery wrenches logic, only to turn a quasi-nihilistic illogic inside out. But the usurper is not a nihilist. Somewhere in Ubu's grotesque depths, he fabricates and believes in a different universe.

The Hamletic aim (to fight life's corruption by playing an opposing game as though in pre-faith) was a legacy, revamped in savage comedy. Legion were authors who adapted similar tensions: Jarry, Apollinaire, Picasso, the surrealists, Vitrac, Ionesco, Salacrou, Beckett, Genet, and Arrabal led the French contingent.

In the twentieth century, tragedy faded. It almost vanishes, in fact, as one scrutinizes theatrical history. Remaining genres' definitions were fuzzy. "Absurd theater," Martin Esslin's coinage, had a steamroller popularity. The concept spread too widely, too fast. Many critics forgot (or did not recognize) that Camus, whom Esslin cited as philosophical fountainhead, had promulgated a very different view in The Myth of

Sisyphus (1942). Camus' "Absurd" is the unchangeable gulf which separates man's striving for Promethean lucidity from the Cosmos' refusal to grant it.

Esslin thus set a bandwagon in motion when he enlarged and changed Camus' idea of the absurd. After 1970, Esslin and a few other critics, scrupulous, recanted slightly; a certain number are more careful about labelling "absurd" any related theater of the epoch.

What of the playwrights themselves? Most did not accept the tag, "Absurdists." Many, indeed, disavowed it categorically. Ionesco, one of the leaders in opposing the term, stated time and again his conviction that "Theater of the Absurd" was an invention of critics, not of playwrights. He specifically named Martin Esslin. As late as 1975, in Dublin, Ionesco restated this belief.[4]

Since King Ubu, Western drama has attracted a bewildering panoply of terms: dark comedy, metatheater, nightmare drama, metaphysical farce, horrendous farce, the self-conscious stage, grotesque theater, black humor plays, anti-theater, Panic theater, the theater of cruelty, theater of ruthless metaphor, etc. Each of these tags has merits. Yet most seem to be deficient in a prime need: overall accuracy.

The eclipse of tragedy in our century is, as we have said, undeniable. (Vestiges prove the rule: O'Neill, Eliot, parts of Lorca, Montherlant, Claudel, Pirandello, perhaps of Miller and Albee.) In devising experimental dramatic forms—often inchoate, though forceful—writers of comedy set out to fill a near-void left in tragedy's decline.

Theater's "savagery" has life-giving ends. This is one of its contradictions, as well as its life blood. It unmasks, then soothes fears which have remained subconsciously repressed. (As we recall, this was a main function of tragedy.) In other arts, the same phenomenon is central. Baudelaire's "damned" poems can cleanse the perspicacious reader, or at least propel

him away from damnation. A Douanier Rousseau painting of a
jungle with serpents sedates our subconscious fears by means
of fantastic harmonics and formful dream. Rhythm's charms may
be a result. Hindemith's crashing tintinnabulations can help to
quiet buried anxieties. Twining in choreographed agonies, sig-
naling the imminence of mortal evaporation, Martha Graham in
dance stimulates hope that we can face excruciating suffering.
Robot-like, King Ubu massacres: we are prepared, through our
hilarity at his antics, to alleviate, in World War II, our nausea at the unspeakable ugliness of Hitler's and Stalin's slaughters.

Quite differently, the Mediterranean--and particularly
Italian--masked carnivals during and after the Middle Ages,
life's game replayed and alive in re-created vitality, allayed
common terrors. Celebrants chased the queasy anxieties derived
from Devil and Lord, everyday suffering, a mate's adultery, old
age and death, powerful rivals, a shrewish wife, disease, the
Plague. Disguised in exultant costumes, revelers before Lent
spurred euphoria via self-forgetfulness. Raucous words flew--
some banned from usual talk.

The Commedia dell'Arte, one of the world's most renowned
semi-improvisatory comic traditions, owed much to these carnival
psychologies and panoplies. Masks, sparse yet stunning, facial
expressions perhaps unmatched since those of ancient Greek theater, extravagant, multi-colored costumes pre-delineated each
character. Dialogue was racy. In its historic beginnings,
improvisation reigned. Ballet-like agility and lightness of
movement were prized. At its best, the Commedia created effects
which ressembled ethereal harmonies, near-dream.

In the Commedia's dramatic tensions, grotesque (at times
diabolical) tangled with debonair traces of divine order. Life's
unchanging dualities (love/fear, hope/despair, joy/sadness,
cruelty/tenderness), had embodiment on stage in sharp, almost
geometrical schemas. Harlequin dancing in roguish triumph

between his two masters choreographs men's prowess in balancing
split loyalties--even those owed to God and Satan.

Savage comedies absorbed pristine impulses from Nature.
Dream-level frights, felt by a spectator, lighten when he iden-
tifies in some sense with forces latent in water, winds, skies,
mountains, woods, tempests, trees, flowers, animals, topography.

A realistic piece of evidence was the night-spectacle of
New York City dowagers around Fifth Avenue who (in safer times)
strolled their dogs around 10 p.m., to help forget old age,
loneliness, boredom, maladies and death for a few minutes.
Flimsy affinity with dogs' vitality assuaged old age's terrors.

Art presents an analogy. It can be balm, intrenchment
against age and disappearance from life. (André Malraux's
esthetic theories are based on this paradox.) Rebellious con-
juration, art's quivers of new life, mentally offset ideas of
death and oblivion.

After King Ubu's reign of carnage in 1896, savage theater
took on unprecedented themes: the sad, sometimes barbarous
clown, dread of technological monsters--atomic and hydrogen
bombs, murderous group'isms, finally proliferation's horrors:
harbingers of one final cosmic explosion.

The forest wolf of children's fables had metamorphosed
into Shakespeare's "universal wolf," capable of devouring
everything, including us all, together with our seemingly
flawed Cosmos, no longer interpretable as earth-centered or
man-oriented.

Comedy, from ancient Greece and Rome through Shakespeare's
Elizabethan Age to frivolous French farces during the nineteenth
century--Feydeau, Courteline, and popular boulevard farceurs--
appeared to be, by and large, a definable genre. Comedy's
typical rhythm, crescendo of complications, and ending, victor-
ious rejoicing in love's hegemony, heroic exaltation, now and
then mock-heroic "empyrean" apogees, were near-impossibilities
once King Ubu's bombshell of rapacity burst on stage.

Optimism, legends of virtuous love, illusions of order in
denouements were henceforth archaic lies. The most laughable
plays often had undercurrents of skepticism. (Feydeau the
effervescent farceur, Courteline, the surrealists, Giraudoux,
Anouilh, Pinter were not exempt.) An incipient monster in man
crept onto stage, clearer, clearer.

About 1885 in France, faith in science, an aging idol,
was deflating. Medical technology, after Ubu and 1896, was no
longer an implicitly trustworthy God. Alfred Jarry's scurrilous travesty on the queasiness of a new Cosmos played a role.
A precocious, scandal-loving Breton, Jarry pricked theater's
most cherished bubbles: tenets of symmetry and balance, plot
staying in linear paths, characterizations outlined in psychological layers, rational language, form reflecting lucidity.

King Ubu controverted practically all these cornerstones
of theater. A concealed motif was the menace of a world tyran-
nized by technology and by idiotic wars. Ubu's notorious,
inward-imagining definition of growing-toward-inhuman omens
resounded in a mock battle cry: "Merdre!" Obsession, metaphysical curse derived from gods of medicine, science, government?
As the farce unfolds, only to splinter, it seems to suggest all
these, simultaneously. Ubu can not help uttering his impreca-
tion, his motto. It belongs to him; it is his emblem, his

14

primal outlook. If the ineffectual adversaries that surround Ubu
are "merdre" too, why not massacre them when the instant avails?

In King Ubu's ludicrous, anti-deistic nausea, Jarry conveys
his own disgust with politics, ethics, esthetics. He adds an
attack on mechanistic concepts of the body, dubious theories
espoused by scientists since modern medicine began. Rebellious
at stringent medical practices, Jarry burlesques idolatry of
surgery in <u>King Ubu</u> and the sequel plays. In atrocious foresight, operations on brain and central nervous system are shown
as sadistic. Farcically, each brain surgery is parodied as
delectable dissection, as gratuitous killing. Savage comedies
were to depict Science as potential murderer and atomic monster.
Thus a savior-mythology was slowly sabotaged.

Hamlet, probing being's pros and cons in an off-the-track
Cosmos, reverberated in European and American savage plays. In
one light, Ubu himself is a pseudo-Hamletic figure. He kills
less to usurp than to plumb the lowest reaches of his terror-
ist's ego. In the 1920's and 1930's, Anouilh's heroes, recoiling
in aversion from life's hypocrisy-requiring taints, Salacrou's
in-part-surreal clowns and quizzical lovers who slide into murder echo Hamlet's gray-black views of existence.

Shakespearean comedy left lines of theater in France. <u>A</u>
<u>Midsummer Night's Dream</u> is one example. No fragile thread of
fancy, this fairy-dream is a warp of love's charades, its shifts
from subconscious to conscious optics. In these figurative
leaps, transcending previous theatrics of revery and artistry
hand in hand in life, Shakespeare foresaw Pirandello, Anouilh,
Genet, Albee, and many others.

Giraudoux owed a debt to Shakespearean mask structures
[life refiltered as love's panoply versus exploiters' parade
of greed, in the <u>Madwoman of Chaillot</u> (1945) transmitted through
irony, caricature, and a subtle species of gaiety]. Unforgettable is the lovely reawakening scene just before the end of
another fantasy, <u>Intermezzo</u>. Everyday noises symphonically

save the heroine from death. One of Giraudoux's most brilliant masque episodes is the mock-victorious procession of oil magnates, pimps and whores down a stairway into oily Hell, the climax of The Madwoman.

Anouilh's deft masterpiece, Thieves' Carnival, orchestrates a life/robbery/love triple metaphor emulating Shakespeare's adroitly-layered whimsies.

Falstaffian tones were heard in other savage comedies. Ghelderode, plunging into situations of lust, foolishness and temptation, still pursued these sonorities. Ionesco, on occasion, was attracted by similar wavelengths of exuberance which recall Falstaff. Ribald, Aristophanic comedy appeared in guises of dissonance: Genet's The Balcony (1956), Arrabal's "Panic Plays," Ghelderode's and Crommelynck's Belgian farces.

The cuckold found metaphorical renewal in Anouilh, Salacrou (even, seriously, in Claudel's Partage de Midi, 1906). It was unfortunate that Lysistrata's saltiness engendered few modern heirs. The twentieth century's queasiness upset erotic, triangular, and quadrangular variants created by Aristophanes or Shakespeare.

Classic conventions for finales of comedy (plenitude, exultation) were obfuscated, if not overthrown. "Comedy of the Empyrean," dizzy euphoria of the sort Molière built in The Would-Be Gentleman, tended to fade. (Ionesco was an exception.) In The Bald Soprano (1953), spectators saw to their bewilderment the victory of self-inventing, unruly language (the real "hero" of the play's splintering fantasies).

Innovative language was in fact a dynamo, energizing imagery. Impulse for a number of savage comedies, it helped to loosen the throttleholds maintained by rules of character, situation, dramatic mode, and genre.

Can we ascribe generic tags to Giraudoux's The Madwoman of Chaillot, Sartre's No Exit (1944), Genet's The Maids (1954), Mrozek's Tango (1965), Pinter's The Homecoming (1965), or Albee's

16

Who's Afraid of Virginia Woolf (1963)? In large degree, each comedy resists strict categorization. Each, in its distinct way, is an act of artistic defiance, meant to stand or fall by its unique idiom, its ambience.

Pyrotechnic, verbal trickery was given new energies by Ionesco, Genet, Pinter, and Albee after the surrealists of the 1920's. Ionesco's bolt into the blue of upside-down language, *The Bald Soprano*, forged a potent theatrical instrument. Long fallow, it moved into guerilla lines of stage esthetics about 1950. Fabricated, self-deluded language was certainly a metaphor of the atomic age's anxieties and ineffectualities.

Themes, in savage comedy, were likewise fertile. They were often radical as well. Deeper than Ubu's plans to obliterate the adversary emerged wild hyperboles for the theater. Many were anti-psychological disclosures of character. Anthropomorphism and metaphors of disintegration escaped psychology's clichés.

More often than not, observed in derision, love soured. (Ghelderode, wild and excessive as he showed love turning into rottenness, Anouilh in minor-key pastiches of degradation, Genet, Arrabal, even Giraudoux sent love's sparkle down the drain. Pinter manhandled and twisted it almost beyond recognition. Love wedded dread in several of Albee's plays. But one of comedy's oldest tensions persisted: could love, if purged, restraighten belief's pillars, making them stronger than before?

Exaltation in *amours* and delight in the bounties of life, ancient comic assumptions, lost sway in savage comedy after 1896. In the years following *King Ubu*, new types of exhiliration began. Rejecting the linearity of structure and logic inherited from classic Greece and Rome, Alfred Jarry inserted in Ubu an aberrant life-direction impulse, ungoverned by divine forces. One main scene in the farce is Poland. War in Ubu's "Poland" has less substance than has vacuous dream. It approaches arbitrary abstraction. One strains to imagine an unbelievable, metaphorical no-man's-land where Ubu is not seriously threatened, a war outside geography. Its imagery forces us to envision a figurative sinkhole of human strivings.

If Jarry had intended a linear travesty, with plot glued inside mathematically clear image and characterization, the whole accomplishment would have been a non sequitur. A line from nowhere to where? When a battle beyond the confines of geography is implied, why pretext dividing lines?

In Ubu's far-away world, arbitrariness must be dominant. It (not bear or enemies) is the ultimate tyrant. Ubu has no existential choice: he can do nothing but persevere as he is, semi-monstrous, grotesque omen of what will happen to man.

Yeats' quip, "After us the savage King!" foretells this, without quite clarifying its awfulness. We can suppose what might have occurred if all avant-garde playwrights in Western Europe and the United States had tried to follow Jarry. Standardized comedies of love, perpetuated by Neil Simons everywhere, would have been denounced as bogus.

Dramatic symmetries were harder molds to shatter. Farces and "well-made" plays of 1880-1910 had calculated, neat patterns of intrigue. Yet a half-decade earlier, Alfred de Musset's dramas, often asymmetrical and unclassical (e.g. Lorenzaccio's rough-hewn, neo-Shakespearean clashes in tone, scene, language and action) eventually became favorite nineteenth-century repertory at the Comédie-Française, eclipsing the popularity of productions by Hugo, Dumas fils, Scribe, Feydeau, and others.

About 1875, seeds of asymmetry started to sprout. (Shakespeare and Musset furnished examples. It is curious that both had shocked French tastes, during generations of misunderstandings.)

When Ubu's dissonant "Merdre!" rang out to launch King Ubu on stage, a slow outgrowth of new theatrical ideas was taking shape. On one plane, disgust with man as he saw himself expanded. "Merdre!" is Jarry's scatalogical overstatement of what outrageous, incipient brute and killer somehow felt himself to be.

The body's depravity was nothing new in farce. It had been a constant medieval theme. With astonishing intensity, Jarry twisted this knowledge to fit his mysterious metaphysical infrastructure, linked to semi-barbarism. The playwright incredibly mocked medical science. King Ubu and sequel plays voice the body's outcry, its unheard revulsions. In ferocious episodes, the central nervous system is wrenched out; brains spill. Jarry is foreshadowing surgical abuses of our day: lobotomies, changes in brain, nerves, longevity.

Enfant-terrible of Parisian literary salons, Jarry interrelated two non-allied twentieth-century deities: war and medicine. King Ubu personifies the inane desire for war which has subjugated man. Seen in this light, his carnage ("Down the traphole with the nobles") is logical. Fatal brain surgery is an instrument in medicine's technological war on men. Human victims are its helpless but indispensable fodder. Surgical science is a form of war, in Jarry's figurative thought.

When Jean Vilar's Théâtre National Populaire performed King Ubu as a musical farce in Paris, Vilar chose as musical leitmotiv Ubu's "Song of Debraining." The theme plunges toward an abyss. Its fearfulness corrodes the whole comedy. Unsettling analogies align warmaking with love, politics, national crises of identity, science, and art.

With burlesqued monstrosity, Ubu threatens to debrain Mère Ubu, as he apes King Medicine, symbol of universal panaceas. Decades later, Henri Bergson, then Einstein, followed by astronomers and physicists, were influential in weakening faith in the assurance of a sure, mechanistic Cosmos. However desperately people tried to cling to archaic idols, these began to crumble. In the arts, revolts multiplied. Cubism, surrealism, concepts of time telescoped (Joyce, Proust, Apollinaire, Faulkner, Picasso), ubiquitous perceptions of space, and so on.

Tchekhov, Strindberg and Pirandello each exerted extraordinary impacts on Western theater. Love's searing ambiguities came to view. Reshaped, the rapacity of love's wars invaded savage comedy after 1920. New amorous puzzles arose from outlandish comic imagery. Freud's hate-love fusions became more and more acute. At times, these were a species of guerilla erotics ending in death (Anouilh, Ionesco, Arrabal, Salacrou). Inner schisms cast doubt on cosmic comprehensibility (Jarry, Dürrenmatt, Mrozek, Lenormand, Anouilh, the fatalistic half of Giraudoux, Pirandello, Albee).

THREE: RIPOSTE

Before 1900, telling counterattacks were set in motion to erode pragmatic and positivistic thinking (Taine, Comte, Renan) and the upsurge of sciences such as psychology. In French literature, Rimbaud, Nerval, Lautréamont, Flaubert, Claudel and Jarry typified the attackers. About a generation later came rebellions led by scientists. Oppenheimer and other atomic physicists in the United States radically challenged assumptions on which science relied (i.e., free enquiry has to be pursued to its ends if scientific results in research are to be validated).

In virtually every science, research raced ahead with unprecedented speed. Discoveries turned old theories topsy-turvy. From 1943 to 1973, more progress was made in physics than in all previous history. This speed was inevitable. Time and Space, translated in literature, were seen anew by scientists, inspired by the findings of Einstein and others. Theories of Space evolved, rapid, portentous.

Temporal/spatial relationships imbedded in new configurations in virtually all the arts (Rodin, Debussy, Rouault, Stravinsky, Klee, Cendrars, Gide, Apollinaire, Proust) were crucial. It appeared that the new century had found its own techniques to hint at enigmas implicit in evolution. Instead of "logical" time sequences, artistic revolutionaries devoured time chunks forwards, backwards, and sideways, not unlike Rilke's imagistic dog.

Sleight-of-hand temporal tricks, leaps at surprising angles increased. (After 1950, films used these devices as stock-in-trade.) "Whirligig" circles, notations of time in reverse, created startling, often beautiful effects [Rimbaud's Bateau Ivre, Apollinaire's La Chanson du Mal-Aimé, Lenormand's Time is a Dream (1919)].

Nourished on Nietzsche's ideologies as a young student in

Paris, also affected by Baudelaire, Strindberg, Tolstoi and Dostoievsky, H.-R. Lenormand was France's most notable avant-garde playwright from 1917 to 1927. Several of his dramas intimated prophecy. A l'Ombre du Mal (1924), Asie, and Le Simoun (1920) portray ethnic battles and the disasters of miscegenation in Africa and Asia. Time is a Dream enigmatically foreshadows the increasing lassitude and self-dissatisfaction of evolving Western civilization. La Folle du Ciel fantasizes mystic-erotic, full-blooded animism in a hunter-seagull mating. The first important French plays to warn of psychoanalysis and its uncharted dangers for patients were Man and his Phantoms (1924) and The Dream-Eater (1922).

Like Anouilh (whose fame began in Paris theaters about 1930), Lenormand developed mastery of darkly astringent comedy. This astringency, too commonly interpreted as dourness or pessimism (e.g., the repute of Anouilh's Waltz of the Toreadors became mired in this cliché) was integral in savage comedy's tones. Though misunderstood during his career, Lenormand indicated paths that later dramatists followed.

King Ubu had abraded nerves by brutishness combined with illogical juvenilism. His wantonness, too, palls before the farce ends. His slipperiness is elusive, weird. Twisted nightmares, gist of the farce, bludgeon audiences into uncertainty, into counterpointed laughter. In the conclusion, something almost nauseous remains..

Surface derision clashes with what is beneath: uneasy doubt and questioning. Jarry's play, revolutionary in this respect, stirs up and aggravates queasiness. All in all, King Ubu is no mirthful buffoon.

Jarry's artistic purpose was unusual. Just as clearly was it human, in the widest sense. War and killing can contort to take grotesque, figurative shapes. The paradox is verified all too often in life and on stage. Efforts to suppress it as "unpleasant" are vain. The agonies of death can evoke laughter, if theatricalized, wrenched from normal moorings, isolated from usual contexts, reshaped in unearthly light. After King Ubu's willy-nilly bloodlettings (or, en masse, his hyperbolic abyss-murders), abstractions of rapacity, a "savage" comic esthetics, drawing away from standard gods of theatrical mythology, was logical.

A half-century later, a summit was touched. Dürrenmatt, the Swiss-German playwright, slashed at traditions in religion, theology, applied science, and social morality. His unpredictable plays (The Visit, The Physicists, The Meteor) undermined cant, theology, and hypocrisies mouthed by the self-righteous (mercantile, political, social, scientific). In far-reaching savage comedies, Dürrenmatt tore at science's and philosophy's presuppositions.

Nor was rollicking farce free of anti-establishment corrosiveness. In secret, subversion now and then lurked. Beginning with the heyday of Feydeau in the 1890's, French farceurs lampooned sanctities: family cohesiveness, love, ambition, the drive for money, position, status, the sacredness of work. While these farces purportedly accepted society's structures, free-spirited heroes implicitly vaunted disloyalties.

Farce's outward bubbles of high living are often deceptive. About 1890, disquiet seethed underneath Feydeau's and Courte-line's social frothiness. In reality, these farces hinted disenchantment with France's insouciance. Scandals (Stavisky, Boulanger, Dreyfus) had rocked opinion. Zola and others had exposed festers on the national conscience. Confidence in France's military inviolability sank. French destiny seemed to totter.

The so-called "belle époque" paradoxically seeped out skepticism and fears for Western Europe's future. Creators in the arts, especially cubists and surrealists, conveyed splinters of this new Angst. After 1900, savage comedies played a part in subverting long-upheld moralities. In France, their authors followed eminent forerunners. Most had not been playwrights, however. They were poets (Nerval, Rimbaud, and Lautréamont, seer of monstrous couplings), short-story tellers and novelists (Flaubert, Mérimée, Villiers-de-l'Isle-Adam, Bloy, Maupassant). Segments of the imagistic and nightmarish characterizations in savage comedy had been foreshadowed before 1895 during the symbolist revolt, led by poets and playwrights. Maeterlinck's, Villiers-de-l'Isle-Adam's, and Claudel's vaporous milieux, their cloudy heroines haunted by dilemmas left in never-never lands were motive thematics which provoked repercussions in dark comedies after 1900.

Symbolism's advances in drama and poetry opened fresh artistic avenues. In all the arts, long-standing status quos crumbled. The premises of orthodox religions and psychology, the inviolability of family ties, the inflexibilities of social structure and its tenets came under serious attack. Some gave way; many changed form, slowly or rapidly.

New generations and revolutions supplanted the old in Western European and American theater. France often blazed the trails. After Apollinaire, precursor of genius, came the surrealists of the stage, mainly in the 1920's: Tzara, Breton, Soupault, Radiguet, Aragon, Salacrou, Vitrac, Artaud. Today, few of their surreal plays survive on or off stage. One outstanding savage comedy, Vitrac's Victor ou les Enfants au Pouvoir, has endured amazingly well, with revivals on Parisian stages throughout recent decades. Others cling to life in anthologies. A few, not easily available in entirety, can be glimpsed in scattered, at times scintillating scenes.

Chronologically, Cocteau and Lenormand belonged to the generation in Paris which included most of the surrealistic playwrights. Not without some affinities with the surrealists, Cocteau persistently disavowed their codified esthetic. He denied affiliation with the group itself. Though highly fanciful, Cocteau's plays do not feature the sliced-up rhythmic beat or the esoteric linguistic caprices of a Tzara or an

Aragon, for example. Cocteau's bizarrely translucid plots, imagery and language differentiate his dramas from those by doctrinaire surrealists.

In 1927, Jean Giraudoux was the main gleam on the Parisian theatrical horizon. Anouilh, his young admirer, arrived a few years later as a luminary. The author of Antigone and Thieves' Carnival was soon to become a leading innovator in savage comedy.

Critics have berated Anouilh for many reasons. His reputation has suffered, perhaps unjustifiably. But Anouilh's plays do carry the lasting mark of a master craftsman. Anouilh had few peers in France or elsewhere as full-bodied, lifelong savage-comedy dramatist.

About 1950 emerged one after another the world-influential triumvirate, Genet, Beckett, and Ionesco. A decade later, Fernando Arrabal, Spanish refugee living in Paris, had a quick splurge of successes, which echoed, attenuated, in England and the United States. Writing in French, Arrabal differed drastically from the previous three dramatists. His alienated psyche, born in Franco's Spain, showered grotesque dreams on Parisian stages.

Thornton Wilder's American fantasy, The Skin of our Teeth, tossed out more than a few grains of savage comedy's ambivalent omens. In tone, the play is far from savage. Yet its time-juggling and whimsy still baffle audiences. (When a production appeared in Paris during the 1950's, the French were confused.) However, Wilder's underlying prophecy is unmistakeable. The little man (the everyday inventor) will prevail, when pushed against the wall of universal catastrophe. (Similarly optimistic, in Nobel Prize speeches, were Faulkner and Camus.)

Before 1945, nuclear bombs and the untold dangers of fission loomed. From Bohr to Einstein to Oppenheimer and beyond, many conscientious physicists warned of atomic cataclysm. Who listened? Who read the Bulletin of Atomic Scientists, designed to alert the public? Not many. Much of the savage comedy since

123,641

25

1945 (Ionesco, Beckett, Albee, Dürrenmatt, Pinter, Mrozek)
attempts to penetrate this inured deafness.

FOUR: SCIENCE AND IMAGINATION CROSSED--
SAVAGE COMEDY AND ITS TRANSGRESSIONS OF RATIONAL FRONTIERS

Alfred Jarry, partly in sardonic playfulness, launched a
new quasi-science: "Pataphysics." Its a-logical charm has
extended far and long. In Paris the whimsical-serious "Collège
de Pataphysique," attracting eminent and highly esoteric thinkers (Ionesco, Vian, Queneau), still held sway in 1975, seemingly
effervescent as ever. Pataphysics, which aims to upend rigid
notions of reasonableness, could be called a psycho-linguistic
virus implanted in logic's brain. It is the science of illogic.
Its viral effects have been potent. After 1896, supra-rational
discoveries suffused literature and the plastic arts. The most
celebrated movement, surrealism, was not alone in its tidal-wave
force.

Demands for translucent psychology in theater were dissip-
ating little by little after the ethereal baths of symbolism.
As faith in science, a man-made God, subsided, spectators grew
less confident in absolutes. Esthetics, like religion and
science, had to find new techniques. Ubu's devastating mockery
of brain surgery and its victim signalled a wide range of
revolts.

Jarry's exacerbated Angst, sketched as Ubu poises unknowingly over an empty chasm, no remedy in sight, is a foreshadowing stance which left marks in twentieth-century playwrights.
Demi-gods were disappearing. Many old beliefs were frittering
away. Empirical "facts" themselves were increasingly cast into
doubt as reassuring guides for men's acts. About 1900, Euro-
peans and Americans began to sense a harassing void. If science,
religion, society, and the infant social sciences were all shaky
premises, rather than demiurges, uncertainty grew. How to fill
the void, how to begin?

Twentieth-century playwrights, like other artistic creators, did their best to "revive" artifacts and impulses which had come from atavistic ingredients in savagery. (Painters and sculptors found their latent "savageries" in African figurines, masks, colors, dances; composers paid heed to tribal and ceremonial music. New Guinea aborigines inspired linguists, writers, and musicians.) Not mainstreams on the surfaces of modern plays, these impressions are variegated, in less-than-lucid motifs which still belong indelibly to savage comedy. Ferocious imageries, to rock problematical gods' pedestals.

Henceforth under artistic bombardment, the frontiers of reason lost distinctness and definable substance. Drama's psychological transparencies from preceding centuries slid toward queasy, waveringly-fearful illogicality.

Tempos accelerated toward possible frenzy, an intrinsic part of certain comedies since Plautus and Aristophanes. These gained new rights in Feydeau's farces. Speed was by the 1890's a mode and structure of uninhibited comic theater. Modern times, with their frenetic worries, were knocking at the door. Speed was a mask. Beneath it lay doubt. In drama, the dawn of the twentieth century was not the mirror of a carefree, high-spending, adulterous belle époque. It was suspicion that the roots of society and life were withering, going sour, in both fathomable and unfathomable ways. On stage, breakneck speed was an attempt to forget conscience and the self, by farceurs and the public.

Without dizzying pace, farces' plots and "ideas" were exactly what scrutiny revealed; they were silly. In the audience, this speed conferred giddy, momentary belief, perhaps trust. Breakneck dialogue and situations suspended a spectator's judgment. This device, giddy pace carried toward frenzy by unaccustomed language, was a staple in some savage comedies (Ionesco's, most of all).

Speed, related to space and line, pervades the arts in the twentieth century. Apollinaire's poems (La Chanson du Mal Aimé), Picasso's experimental, cubist sculptures and semi-hypnotic paintings of tattered concepts were exemplary. Klee, Stravinsky and countless others achieved comparable effects with kinetic speed, as it revolutionized form and linear thinking. Picasso, for one, anticipated this technique in the century's esthetics.

Light-hearted exuberance and gaity, visible in French fin-de-siècle theater and art, seemed to dissipate gradually after 1896. A dark, derisory underside had emerged in Ubu and in Villiers-de-L'Isle-Adam's foreboding, mystical works. Anouilh's biting comedies were to bring this somberness to a climax. Some of the prefigurations were circuses' fantasmagoric tinges (much admired by Picasso and literati of his day), shootings in surrealistic comedies, Lenormand's ethnic uprisings, Salacrou's mystery-contorted characters wandering through love's culs-de-sac.

Black-shadowed irony spread. Disenchanted heirs of Hamlet, Falstaff, and Quixote, savage comedy figures from Ubu to Vitrac's giant child, Giraudoux's eloquent ragpicker, Anouilh's déclassés and hunchbacks to Arrabal's amorphous, sex-flouting grotesques, spew out their obsessive disappointments and, in the end, their futilities, as they try to combat a sense of cosmic miasma.

Futility is savage comedy's dissonance. It may be its ultimate metaphor. Fantasmagoria also participates. Especially in France, surrealistic poetry combined analytical data and self-exploration in new depths (medicine, psychiatry, mathematics, philosophy, the graphic arts, botany, war) with imagination's wildly-flying splinters. These elements very often portrayed a comic figure from within his secret, psychic recesses. Anti-heroes like Michaux's Plume or Anouilh's Bitos, quixotically revolting without knowing which directions to take, burlesque seers of dehumanization and technology's stampede such as Charlie Chaplin's baffled foe of machines' tyranny in the movie, Modern Times, embodied ludicrous Angst.

Lacking tragedy, the century's playwrights, artists and musicians had to revamp the strategies of comedy. (Beckett's legerdemain with language and quasi-slapstick gamesmanship and imagistic tricks with objects such as Lucky's rope in Waiting for Godot showed how comedy can haunt us with universal, perhaps cosmic befuddlement.)

About 1915, French theatrical gaiety fell unconnected, loosed as if from its moorings. Disjoined, it rollicked in Apollinaire's spoof on increasing the birthrate, The Breasts of Tiresias (1917), Picasso's semi-erotic Desire Caught by the Tail (1945), and Cocteau's Les Mariés de la Tour Eiffel (1921). Amorous highjinks shifted into danger in rampaging surrealistic comedies by Desnos and Aragon, poet-dramatists of the 1920's.

Roger Vitrac, master of pseudo-juvenile satire, helped turn comedy's esthetics toward outrageous, ironic cruelty. A new comic wellspring gushed out. Victor ou les Enfants au Pouvoir (1924), his best-known satire, was one of a few plays of the era to attract large audiences in Paris as late as the 1960's. Acute, laughably somber, almost apocalyptic, Vitrac's savage play prophesied youngsters' enmity with parents, forty years before "generation gap" crises became full reality. About 1927, ferocious dramatic suppositions of this sort were dislodging frivolity as a pervasive obsession of French comedy.

Anti-social vitriol as imagistic weapon, inherent in Vitrac's caricatures of bumbling older generations and idiotic traditionalists of every age, reappeared about a decade later in Anouilh's wry comedies (including those slightly mislabeled as "pink.")

Anouilh casts society in an abrasive role. It blocks forgiveness of rebellious individualism. On both sides, vengefulness impels slashes and counter-slashes. Anouilh's plays summon up riposte, counterattack. Finances, art, love, marriage, social status, infidelities reek with laxity and cowardice. Spurious social veneers and degradation abound. Anouilh, whose optimism was scarred during his youth, when he accompanied his elder's third-rate music tours and rubbed against tawdry intrigues, reiterated a metaphor that came to possess him: on every level, finances are stench. They infect us all.

Relatively unknown outside France, Armand Salacrou rivalled Anouilh in scathing comedies. Histoire de Rire (No Laughing Matter, 1939), a sardonic comedy-drama of impossibly tangled loves, creates a less blatant disenchantment than Anouilh's. Salacrou anticipates the seamier edges of social flux, even in the most likeable characters. Four attractive friends are pitched into a net of jumbled dreams and envies. The result is violent death, nearly unpredictable. Aspirations, mores beyond control are the culprits. While Anouilh castigates, Salacrou seems to cry out in sudden amazement. His characters, however, only now and then match the power of Anouilh's predators and uncapitulating prey.

Satire and dark wonderment are Salacrou's forte. L'Inconnue d'Arras, very ingenious in form, leads a spectator through blind alleys to an explosive dénouement, almost incredible.

Mysteriousness, joined to anti-logic, fills Salacrou's early comedies (Poof, 1947, and Circus Story, 1922), enhanced by frolicksome surrealism and a joyous, youthful plot's quick leaps. Salacrou's impact lasted from about 1925 to 1960 in France. Depiction of love's fantasies tied sardonically to the unknowable was his chief mark of individuality.

Fascination with the psyche's enigmas was spurred and shaped during the decades 1935-1955 by Georges Neveux and Supervielle, and some ten years later by Schéhadé, Boris Vian, Arrabal, and others. Among its new dramatic devices was mystification (in French, purposeful sleight-of-hand with characters and situations).

More than twenty years after Salacrou's stormy capers and surrealistic plays, which toyed with logic, mystification and broken-lined characterization sprouted full bloom with Ionesco during the 1950's in French theaters.

The Bald Soprano (1953), bizarrely heralding a new comic era, assembles other-worldly countenances and dynamics. The Smiths and the Martins only seem to be half-normal figures of comedy. Something is missing; something, on the other hand, is total excess. They are not "thick" in dramatic potential. Their dialogue spins, returns, top-like. Their sparks of inevitability are hidden beneath a layer of figurative tricks: inane cycles of metaphor, spouting of clichés, voltage-packed pieces of new language. Expectable psychologies have gone out the window. Linguistics contorts characters.

A maid-not-quite-maid recites an obsessed jingle about fire. Fire is everywhere. It leaps verbally. Yet it is never visible. A fireman arrives. He is avid to fight fires not yet started. With fresh comic necessity, poetically, language explodes as the apotheosis of The Bald Soprano. In this "explosion," a giant language's fire-bomb, the semi-logical climax of incendiary danger, awakening exuberance, is a radical new comic presage. Originally sealed inside language's secrets and feints, fearful laughter breaks out.

Menace of destruction (especially that of death) is Ionesco's primordial theme. It structures his important plays. Ionesco transposes dangers that recur time after time: conformism's binding irons, social rhinoceritis, decrepitude, treachery, domestic shrewishness, pestilence, tyrannies of war and stultification.

These are life's worst mystifiers, its rampaging beasts. Rhinoceros (1960) thrusts us abruptly into mob psychosis. The deathly vertigo of pseudo-knowledge and the idolatries of theory without substance give ghastly tones to Rhinoceros, The Lesson (1950) and L'Epidémie ou Jeux de Massacre (1970). In Exit the King (1967), Ionesco's favorite anti-hero, Bérenger, wears the crown, as he has for centuries. Fugue and counterpoint, intricately paradoxical, harmonize the king's puzzled interminglings of remembered delights and terrors of mortality. He faces death instant by instant. _Joie de vivre_ and dread mottle, combine.

Rejecting scientific and religious dogmas, Ionesco bared his puzzlement, his almost ever-present fear. On stage, as in _The Bald Soprano_ and _Jacques ou la Soumission_ (1955), metamorphoses of characters, attitudes, metaphors placed in weirdly elegiac juxtapositions hinted at life's quirks, its being sliced into bits. Dream's fearfulness was omnipresent. Little wonder that Ionesco's comidies bewildered spectators for several years. With the success of _Rhinoceros_ in 1959, his world-wide fame was launched.

Imagistic hoax (_mystification_), a thematic wool spread over the spectator's eyes, twisted awesome, death-dealing motifs. Adapted from surrealism (Ionesco began as fantasmogoric poet), anti-Aristotelian and anti-Cartesian techniques of counter-logic invaded the theater.

Apollinaire's Tirésias, prefiguring the surreal, had spoofed sex transfer, in a history-making and prophetic characterization. Tirésias' breasts turn into gigantic balloons and float into the sky. Ages and freed sexes scamper, topsy-turvy.

Victor, Vitrac's virulent child-hero, is over six feet tall and knows secrets of what will happen, baffling his elders. Poems of surrealism had already been full of similar derision and frivolous hoaxes. Whimsical and somber united. The combination threw brilliant sparks.

In the 1920's, theatrical _percées_ probed hitherto masked instincts. An acidic humor pervaded savage plays. When Anouilh gained ascendancy on Paris stages during the early 1930's, dark comedy had begun to produce rather distinct sub-species. In most of these, a corrosive, comic stance prevailed. It was durable. Savage comedy's eccentricities outlasted a majority of the contemporaneous styles of comedy. Tragedy was slowly dying. Light-hearted farce _à la Feydeau_ could always be seen in Paris theaters. But very few farces stood the test of time. Serious dramas, of course, continued. By 1960, musicals and

frothy comedies won favor again. By 1970, substantial drama
was a reduced part of Parisian offerings.

Friedrich Dürrenmatt, the Swiss-German author, was the most
visionary of the mid-century's savage dramatists. In certain
ways, he was a prototype. Son of a pastor, Dürrenmatt undermined systematic theology, sought to make its foundations quiver, if not topple. Vehemently, he sabotaged self-serving
sciences and technologies.

Claire ("lucid"), barbaric heroine of The Visit (1956),
incarnates quasi-animal ruthlessness. Little does she care if
she spoliates a town's moral base when she takes vengeance
against a former lover, who is no more than a puny victim.
Claire's lust as destroyer has full sway.

Dürrenmatt's most profound phobia, the unchecked cycle
that leads us to cosmic explosion, guides The Physicists (1961).
Madmen or geniuses? The play's not-quite heroes, scientific
theorists emprisoned in an enigmatic asylum for the insane, keep
spectators in mystery. If they are scientists, not lunatics,
they pay a terrifying price. They have bartered thought and
discovery of atomic tomorrows for captivity, with murder their
only means for survival.

Will nationalistic power-grabs and espionage of cosmic
secrets implicit in the atom, will the universe's disclosures
of omnipotence in new findings protect "mad" thinkers? The
Physicists vitalizes this question. The play is ferocious in
rebellion against official mind-control and atomic nationalism.

Militarism's deceit and police-state killings due to bumbling come under metaphorical whiplashings. Though a bit fuzzy
on its surfaces, deliberately puzzling, an unrelenting counterattack on vacuous modern group-think, The Physicists is a masterpiece of foreboding. The savage comedy's prophecy, its accuracy clearer and clearer, dismays. Dürrenmatt's later plays
(Visit to a Strange Planet, The Meteor, Play Strindberg) create
similar, fiercely premonitory drama, with dilemmas insinuating

perils in planetary disarray.

Central figure in The Meteor, Dürrenmatt's perplexing play (Der Meteor, 1966), Schwitter is an author who clamors to die but rejects life's end. Nobel Prize winner in literature ("drunken, lecherous, mean"), Wolfgang Schwitter is an undecipherable riddle for others and for himself. Dürrenmatt, to clear the angles of approach to his most mysterious characters (including Schwitter), offered the definition "Verschlusselt": interlocked, as in cryptography. This theatrical interdependence of hidden codes, as in espionage, is rare, if not unique. Dürrenmatt's characters such as the imagistic conundrum, Schwitter, are tangled, ravelled. They are, as Dürrenmatt himself has admitted, messages not quite decoded.

Deep inside himself, concealed from all, Schwitter bears a fierce enigma. The spectator sniffs a sort of polyvalence. Without knowing its exact ingredients, he senses that his syndrome (quasi-shapeless, primal dissonance in characterization and plot) impels a new kind of savage comedy.

With variations, Albee, after Jarry and the surrealists, used similar dynamics: unions of irreconcilable discords, sometimes shrieked in what seems to be a bottomless ferocity. Ubu's gruesome, cleft personality in language and act; Martha (Who's Afraid of Virginia Woolf) uttering catastrophically split faiths (in a prestigious father, a husband without power, a fiasco-prone young geneticist, a son devised by a floundering imagination) are close to the same syndrome.

Ionesco, in fantasm or in a-logical, ghostly expressiveness, concocts different nether realms for his plays. The Bald Soprano, The Lesson, Jacques or the Submission and Rhinoceros transmit Ionesco's unresolved bafflement and terror in a Cosmos going haywire. Warm contact and empathy fade out of twentieth-century life. An obsession of Ionesco's can be discerned in a theme he has repeated many times: a petty argument expands to world disaster, sometimes to world explosion. Intimacy, deformed and

35

misinterpreted, precipitates cosmic splintering. Ionesco's quandary, then, is how to express the most equivocal facets of intimacy without causing estrangement, fire, explosion. (The maid's poem-litany of fire's ubiquitous marvels in The Bald Soprano, not as gratuitous as it seems at first viewing, really insinuates this danger for the Martins and the Smiths.)

In 1970, in a remarkable interview, Dürrenmatt made clear his concept of theater's social and moral function. He underlined his belief that the theater should change man's social possibilities. Savage comedy's long-range comic arrows keep man's eyes alert, as did those of a Shakespeare and an Aristophanes:

"Without art man is blind.
Through the theater the dramatist tries to change the social reality of man...
I write only comedies... ... (My method) is dialectical.
I show the other side...
Aristophanes I like. Shakespeare... (I) adapted Titus Andronicus.
I prefer tightly structured pieces. I also experiment with time..."[1]

One might relate this to Artaud and his credo of cruelty. Critics tended to fail to look beyond his sensationalism and his flagrant mistakes. Artaud, whose highest talents were theory, acting, and poetry, was a very unsuccessful playwright and an erratic director. In the United States, as in Europe, Artaud's influence was an amalgam of luminosity, snobism, and misinterpretation.

"The Theater of Cruelty," Artaud's world-known term, did not call for sado-masochism, brutality, or dismemberment on stage. Nor was bloodshed a sina qua non. Artaud's simplest definition was, "Everything that acts is cruelty."

Gesture, décors, (if they act on us), physical movement, costumes, accessories, music, poignant silences--all should exert kinetic effects, "cruelly" changing, "transvertebrating" actor and spectator, in Proustian parlance. Cruelty twists our sensations of time, space, personality, rigid identity—with their subtle associations. "Cruel" synthesis of kinetic/esthetic powers was Artaud's aim.

Artaud was a savage rebel against sterile conventions in theater (vocabulary, use of voice and body, plot patterns, themes, poetics, music, dance, clichés in esoteric ethnic sources). He felt compelled to assemble ingredients from untapped lands and arts to create a thunderbolt violence in drama. He sought esthetic jolts. Artaud wanted to purify the theater of laziness.

Antonin Artaud's research in ancient Greek drama, occultisms of Far Eastern philosophies and art, Irish and Mexican-Indian mysticisms, rituals, objects of magic worship obeyed this unflagging impulse. In Balinese ballet and other dances of the East, in little-known music, Artaud thought he had begun to relocate a pristine nexus of theater before its contamination by bourgeois complacency and habit. He sensed ways to fuse dissonant, intricate, wild reveries from unaccustomed art forms. He would worship and transfuse them in "the theater of cruelty."

This ideal was, in fact, abstruse and ethereal. Only in pieces was it ever really used. An unhappy paradox doomed Artaud to deform his theories when he composed his ghastly plays: Spurt of Blood, The Cenci. As art, they failed to last. Historically, they are still curiosities. Spurt of Blood highlighted tortures and an unconvincing, almost ghoulish atmosphere. The Cenci, wildly adapted from Florentine scandal—revenge, family atrocities, murder, incest—is almost as incredible, with dialogue that rarely "acts" on a spectator.

Artaud's most famous disciples besides Barrault (Roger Blin, Jerzy Grotowski, Peter Brook) construed his ideas varyingly. "The theater of cruelty" too often went astray. Only seldom (as in Grotowski's rather abstract ventures to induce physiological nirvana and in Brook's gymnastic-fantastic Midsummer

37

<u>Night's Dream</u> and dreamily erotomaniac <u>The Balcony</u>) did Artaud's wild esthetics come alive on stage.

The potential "living phantasm" powers of actor and troupe, Artaud's goal, remained fouled in the grip of brutish or anthropomorphic "realisms." Artaud's savage vista of theater was unfulfilled, in large part.

Can sustained "cruelty" in anything like Artaud's sense be comic? Artaud himself barely broached this question. His temper choleric, his body wasted by excruciating disorders, he seemed not to be built for comedy. Yet an irony persisted. His theoretical visions colored comic cruelty still to come.

Piercing, unremitting, caustic, unworldly in language and music, ripostes by individuals against society's dictates: Artaud wanted to exploit these paths. He hoped they might lead to "the theater of cruelty." By instinct, Artaud felt committed to rebut the myriad forms of malignancy and repression amassing like an army of virulences in stages of assault. Much of Artaud's creativity was impelled and shaped by suffering. Mortal tortures traversed his body. In counterattack, he transsubstantiated these enemies into extravagant notions of the willfulness of a Cosmos which he saw as cracked, aberrant.

Artaud's little-known poems, barbaric and abstruse, embody a weird cosmogony. They inherently prophesy "cosmic whiplash," post-atomic age wavering and torture inflicted on man, whose forces can never equal those of this world tremor.

From 1930 to 1970, playwrights like Anouilh, Genet, Pinter, Mrozek, Ionesco, Beckett and Arrabal wrote scathing comedies designed to provoke different kinds of dark, squeamish laughter. None fit Artaud's nightmare. Some came close. Psychic omens' shudders quivered in savage comedies of many varieties, understood only in part.

Rapacity (whether mental or physical) is one hallmark of savage comedy. Widespread in Greek tragedy, Shakespeare and Restoration theater, a near-jungle ferociousness gushes back

into French farce in King Ubu. Attenuated (with few exceptions),
it reappears in Western comedy after 1896.

Among Artaud's signal accomplishments was his influence in
helping to rid the serious French stage of trite language. Well-
made but insipid plot patterns also began to lose sway, especially after 1945. Artaud's manifestoes called for rapacious
powers fusing in drama, with the splitting of old barriers in
themes. The goal was an unearthly vibrance in word and act.

But Artaud failed to see a crucial truth. Anyone who tries
to dive into his own depths in defiance of society, chasing chimera in the avenues of "cruelty", exacerbates his humanity. He
makes himself a misfit, a weirdly comic or pathetic figure in
others' eyes. Anouilh, for example, highlights the ludicrousness of a lone rebel in Pauvre Bitos. We chortle wryly at Bitos,
intellectual-political caricature, seen in and by himself. Ironies of inanity start within; in the climax, they burst. After
about 1933 and the plays of Giraudoux's comic maturity (post-
Intermezzo), the most refined forms of savage comedy, often
inward-contorted, pinpointed profound twists of the self barely
intimated in King Ubu.

FIVE: WHIMSY WITH SAVAGE UNDERTONES

Guillaume Apollinaire, one of France's most celebrated poets of the early twentieth century, wrote one epochal play. The Breasts of Tirésias is a friendly satire on the French government's pleas for more babies after the losses of men in World War I. The comedy has an aura of pleasantly salty individualism. Composed in 1903 in large part, only seven years after King Ubu's debut, Apollinaire's joyous farce acquired definitive shape in 1916-1917.

Apollinaire's poem, The Octopus, had sardonically associated the human and the beastly. The link was to emerge in ensuing decades as one focus of savage comedy:

> Jetant son encre vers le ciel
> Suçant le sang de ce qu'il aime
> Et le trouvant délicieux.
> Ce monstre inhumain, c'est moi-même.

> (Launching its ink toward the sky
> Sucking the blood of what it loves
> And finding it delicious.
> This inhuman monster is myself.)[1]

After Apollinaire's whimsies and sex change in The Breasts of Tirésias, comic theater could resemble an unbridled antic: a game, not life's echo. New equations ruled. Apollinaire's farce strips the ideal of naturalism to fragments. After the extravaganza-dream of The Breasts of Tirésias, realistic drama's posture, that of an invented world posing as "natural" on the stage, struck more and more playwrights as a sham.

The vivid game of postulating a play which translates life prismatically as other than life excited young dramatists. Gusto, at times untrammeled, held out promises still unfulfilled. Jarry, who had mocked humdrum capitulation to "normalcy" in the esthetics of comedy, slashed at drama's hidebound habits. In King Ubu, he had concocted an unknowingly exact omen of writhing comedy for the future. Beyond Ubu's masquerade cruelty, it builds a life-view impossible to overlook: supra-lifelike, universal rapaciousness. It is a fixed hyperbole, fringing the absolute.

Unlike existence, savage theater embraced these hypothetical games, which remind us of nightmarish combats. The Breasts of Tirésias, distantly akin to some of the spirit of King Ubu, was gleeful as it cavorted in artistic revolt. One actor personified the whole world. He united dance, acrobatics, primirive and modern origins of noise which seemed futuristic, colors, gestures, painting, poetry, semi-surreal action and décor. Apollinaire's lampoon was an early model for "total theater"—a concept to be popularized beginning about a decade later. At core, the poet joined "joy, voluptuousness and virtue," as he said, in impertinent harmony.

The most revealing location of Ubu's struggles had been Poland, which Jarry termed as indefiniteness: image of anywhere and nowhere, in simultaneous suggestion. The Breasts of Tirésias has a whimsical site: Zanzibar. But it evokes concurrent metaphors: Paris (with its fanciful games of life and spurious pretexts) and our universe, one of oneiric bubbles, most of them about to break. All the same, symbol was not the only trick in the farce's games with fertility.

The heroine, Thérèse, has a blue face. Doldrums? Not so. A friend of Picasso and of other famous painters, Apollinaire may well have been enjoying a lark, poking fun at Picasso's celebrated "blue period" of painting. Perhaps even more important was the likelihood that the playwright was re-releasing childlike desires to paint a face "wrong," with a bizarre color. This type of pristine impulse—reactivated by a mature creator— lies close to the heart of savage comedy extravagance.

Le génie, c'est l'enfance retrouvée à force de volonté, said Baudelaire. Genius realigns, reinvents its own childlikeness. Childhood inclinations, merging ferocity and mockery (asocial sentiments repressed, if not partly purged, in adulthood) are discoverable in the foundations of savage comedy.

41

Thérèse's dress in <u>The Breasts of Tiresias</u> is painted in fruit and monkey motifs. We see, in advance, a primitivistic inspiration, which was to typify certain ferocious comedies of the years 1920-1975.

Metamorphoses multiplied rapidly and uncannily in plays after 1950. Two or three generations earlier, one of the first important transmutations shown on stage was Thérèse's near-change to maleness. Incomplete, if hirsute sex transfer, the ludicrous spectacle was a remarkable foreshadowing of wild change-of-sex scenes portrayed by Arrabal, Ionesco, and others.

Much more than an astonishing trick, sexual reversal was a compulsive metaphor. It came from dread of man's atomic-age mutations, enforced by powers beyond his control. Apollinaire's prophetic farce contained other vanguard techniques: the device of tantalizing and provoking the audience, miracles, animism, and a stage crammed menacingly full with objects. Omens stand out in the play. Not only was it a forerunner of surrealism; it prefigured the bewildering rebelliousness which suffused works by Salacrou, Anouilh, Lenormand, Dürrenmatt, and Albee.

What could have spawned the barbed-wire fearfulness of the "monstrous" theater composed by Dürrenmatt central in mid-century? The Swiss-German author and an interviewer, Violet Ketels, provided a momentous explanation:

Dürrenmatt: ...⌈The world is⌋ ... "something monstrous, a riddle of misfortunes which must be accepted but before which one must not capitulate."

Violet Ketels: ...⌈<u>The Meteor</u> seeks⌋ ... "to reflect the monstrously paradoxical nature of life which, in Dürren-matt's eyes, is brutal, blind, brief, and accidental."[2]

Savage comedy, years before Dürrenmatt's arrival in world theater, had slowly formed an unworldly ideological skeleton:

(1) The irremediable monstrosity of the world is its human/inhuman, unreachable, bewilderingly perilous basis.

(2) Man has to accept the universe's monstrosity.

(3) Life, irreconciliable paradox, is raw happenstance, "brutal, blind, brief, accidental."

(4) A playwright must challenge this cosmic puzzle, this enemy (as a hunter defies a killer-panther). He confronts the enigma of enigmas: the excess speed with which life mutates, its aberrant lust to destroy.

Apollinaire's warning eccentricities in The Breasts of Tirésias indirectly echoed in Pablo Picasso's pseudo-play, Desire Caught by the Tail, some twenty-five years later. Written in three days during the first winter the Germans occupied Paris in World War II (1941), Picasso's fantastic comedy was a success when it was revived in the 1960's. Desire is almost a non-play.

This semi-surrealist, tenuous comedy has been defined as a "painter's recipe." Desire is Occupation hunger, with oneiric visions of food. Picasso has gifts as an imaginative playwright: wild, racing imagery, an artist's lampooning of the theater's stodginess in names, plot, or love. One savage-comedy tendency is notable. Picasso nonchalantly fuses notions of the living and the non-living. This imagistic folly leads one character, Round End, to proclaim, "Men are mad." But the pervasive motif is delirious, non-vengeful madness in fantasmagorical dreams of food. Pablo Picasso, in adroit semi-madness and giddy echo-chamber tricks, anticipated Ionesco's verbal extravaganzas about a decade later. In partial parallels, Ionesco spewed words like an enraged fountain.

SIX: SURREALISM'S SAVAGERY ON STAGE

In poetry, surrealism's dream-level, associative fireworks
are famous. French surrealist plays, often written by poets,
captured many lodes of explosiveness. The 1920's was an extraordinary period for these comedies. Numerous critical surveys
of the genre emerged, notably those by Henri Béhar, Michael
Benedikt and George E. Wellwarth, and J.H. Matthews.

Perhaps too obvious is the link between poetic and theatrical surrealism. Questions remain. Are the two genres really
compatible? What dramatic aims underlie the composition of a
surrealistic play? How must it differ from a surreal poem? On
these problems, confusion lingered.

In The Breasts of Tirésias, a crucial truth was reaffirmed.
Most surrealistic energies, in a poem, seem to flow inward to
redefine one presence, that of a narrator. On the other hand,
a play ostensibly constructs external and social dynamics; a
protagonist's drive is usually socialized, blunted. Many metaphors serve this purpose, that of social frustration.

French surrealists very often had--and hid, in some degree--
acidic outlooks toward society's stagnation. Propositions and
manifestoes were monnaie courante among poets of 1917-1935 generations. The surrealist playwright, no didacticist or pedagogue, seldom an effective agitator in politics, preferred the
unlikely impacts of humor running free, its directions unled.

The visually weird, disjointed or grotesque was staged
with semi-incoherent leaps in plot, as though ahead, backwards,
sideways, upward, downward. Surreal comedy favored obliqueness;
it juxtaposed the intemperate, the violent, the inexplicable,
the wildly accelerated. Now and then the dramatist was entrapped
in some quest or dream of maturing childlikeness. Fantasies on
stage chased psychic cobwebs which had seemed to gather over
long-covered memories. The child's freedoms, spontaneities,

and games might be a guide to new theatrical imagery. To be sure, these bits of the past had frequently been sliced by creators of every kind into splinters, later to be recombined. But these had often been rooted in tradition and similitude. New combinations, less foreseeable and more startling, were sprouting in poets' notebooks.

Surrealistic comedies, cast in "savage" tones, launched sensations of the spontaneous and staccato delights aroused by amazement. Underneath surfaces of capriciousness and grotesqueries lurked future-oriented phobias: (1) growth's speed, causing giddiness; (2) new perceptions of time as jerky, unmeasurable, dangerous spasms; (3) the animal/man/machine linkage, erupting in modernistic nightmare, weirdly anthropomorphic; (4) faster and faster metamorphoses, animal, objectal, and human; (5) man's deformities depicted as savagely hyperbolic; (6) signs of a wobbling Cosmos, outside logic's control.

Omens glinted. Metaphorical highjinks and ruses invented by the surrealists, who prefigured plays by Anouilh, Beckett, Dürrenmatt, Arrabal and Pinter, were some thirty years ahead of the times. The surrealists' preoccupation with one aspect of evolution's growth/deformity/metamorphosis was striking. By and large, critics overlooked the prophecies hidden in this obsession.

Ionesco, whose youthful encounters in Paris with surrealist poets left lasting imprints, admitted that views of metamorphosis filtered into his plays, when he explained The Painting (1955), one of his lesser-known comedies:

"...the theme...is metamorphosis, with which I deal in a parody, in order, through indirection, to disguise its serious nature."[1]

Human transformations, sudden and incredible (including man-animal coupling and men coalescing with various species) were evoked in French poetry of the nineteenth century (Lautréamont, Rimbaud, et al). The surrealists adopted the theme with a vengeance.

During the heyday of surrealist plays in France, 1917-1927, the outstanding playwrights were Louis Aragon, Robert Desnos, André Breton, Philippe Soupault, Raymond Radiguet, Tristan Tzara, Armand Salacrou, and Roger Vitrac.

Other dramatists fringed the "official" tenets of surrealism. Classed too readily with surrealist authors in theater and poetry, Jean Cocteau (whose films were, in several instances, surreal) disavowed both the surrealistic style and the coterie of poets in Paris, refusing to see himself as doctrinaire. A few of his plays, unearthly, still differed in many ways from those of a Tzara or an Aragon.

Cocteau's language has symmetry and cohesiveness; his plots, though eerie in parts, are linear. Artaud is not a categorical surrealist. His Spurt of Blood, produced in 1925, displays his major flaws as well as his deviations from the surreal. Some evolved from, then became differentiated from ideologies of surrealism: shock for the sake of shock, sentimentality inverted toward mawkish suffering, crude lines of plot. Few spectators found Artaud's arbitrary fierceness on stage palatable as drama.

In Tristan Tzara's The Gas Heart (1920), one of the first memorable plays of French surrealism, metamorphosed beings perform (Eye, Mouth, Nose, Eyebrow). One of the most incredible of all stage inventions goes into action: "...the gas heart walks slowly around, circulating widely; it is the only and the greatest three-act hoax of the century; it will satisfy only industrialized imbeciles..."[2]

In a nearly plotless maelstrom, visionary motifs churn up and around, time and again. Fusions of man and non-human recur ("He flattened out like a bit of tin foil...several memories several leaves testified to the cruelty of an impassioned and actual fauna"). We perceive time's quasi-human, wrinkled fabric: "Time wears mustaches now like everyone, even women and shaven Americans. Time is compressed--the eye is weak--but it isn't yet in the miser's wrinkled purse."[3]

The play's hidden motor is time ("Lagging, isn't it...Very lagging, isn't it"). In this seemingly casual jest for theater audiences, Tzara postulates a metaphysical harassment that Beckett was to do battle with in Waiting for Godot thirty years afterward. Time refuses to behave, to let us alone, to stay in line. It enslaves us and our wills.

Tzara's The Gas Heart, with its uncanny poetry telescoping the action, typifies the first full-bodied stream of surrealism on stage. Figuratively, its elements tantalize, unravel. Rationality has been locked outside doors. The key has been lost, in a cache no one knows. And there is no skeleton key that works. If a spectator was unsatisfied, jittery, one of the surrealistic aims was fulfilled: uneasy questioning of what the theater can do and elicit. Symmetry was in collapse. In fright of its life, linearity, self-deluded, faced the cemetery. Theater would never be the same.

A rather small group of surrealist or near-surrealist plays, some practically unstageable, some more whimsical than savage, left imprints historically: Jean Cocteau's The Wedding on the Eiffel Tower (1921), Raymond Radiguet's The Pelicans (1921), If You Please (1920) by André Breton and Philippe Soupault, Louis Aragon's The Mirror-Wardrobe one Fine Evening (1922), Armand Salacrou's A Circus Story (1922), Roger Vitrac's Victor ou les Enfants au Pouvoir (1924), and Artaud's Spurt of Blood (1925) and The Cenci (1964), were an epochal, if erratic gamut for the stage.

Echos of surrealism in the theater recurred in France, in the United States, in England and in other Western countries from 1940 to 1960 in particular. Sometimes the plays were luminous. In France, Robert Desnos, Robert Pinget, Jean Tardieu, Georges Neveux, Armand Gatti, Liliane Atlan and others offered individualistic fantasmagoria. There were small gems: Tardieu's Romeo-Juliet transposition, Les Amants du Métro (1960), for

47

instance, was a masterpiece in continuous understatement in a
familiar scene.

Unlike the majority of large surrealistic canvases for the
theater, Vitrac's best plays were still playable in 1970. _Victor ou les Enfants au Pouvoir_ (1924) is Vitrac's monument of
savage comedy. Its bitter acidity and clear prophecies are
powerful. Vitrac was an artistic heir of Jarry. He renewed
Jarry's ebullience and causticity; above all, his instincts in
drama, like Jarry's, led him to concoct pre-atomic-holocaust
omens, accompanied by deep ruptures among parents and offspring.

A few days before he died, Vitrac cried out in a prediction
to his young wife, "You'll see, how I'll be young!" _Victor_,
issued from tensions born of adolescent and childish candor
attacking elders' lies, is strident. The comedy equates adults'
cowardice with death's nearness. Expostulating in a child's
barbaric fury, Victor, nine-year-old, six-foot hero, renounces
adulthood as rotten with hypocrisy and cowardice. Victor, like
King Ubu, creates salacious new words ("your entails" for "your
entrails") to push satire into savagery. Victor's mythic pre-
monitions (unstoppable war, ruin, a nation split by cowards,
parents dehumanized, children who lose all trust, generations
destroying each other) combine rage and foreboding. These preceded the "Angry Young Men" savagery of John Osborne and fellow
British playwrights by more than twenty years.

Even as hyperbole, Victor (prophetic child-seer of near-
Apocalypse) is unreal and grotesque. This augments his pun-
gency. Too clairvoyant, the giant lad is pitted against ingrown
elders, his antagonists. Dangerously precocious, Victor must
die. He will never fit an adult scheme of things.

Awesome enigmas (Why does youth see straight, cutting
through the falsities which define adulthood? Why does a parent
twist and abandon his children ethically?) rack the comedy. The
elders' delusions and excuses curiously foreshadow Ionesco's

comedies (The Bald Soprano, The Chairs, Rhinoceros, Exit the
King). The black laughter of corrosiveness, however pessimis-
tic its encounter with dread, may be a partial remedy for Hamletic Angst transposed in the twentieth century. Vitrac's humor,
then Ionesco's, led in this transposition into drama of cosmic
wavering.

Foreseen in Victor by means of biting metaphors are youth-
parental conflicts of the 1960's: revolutions in universities
of the United States and elsewhere, the social upheavals caused
by Viet-Nam fighting, bitterness separating two generations,
especially on issues of involvement in war (Victor sees his
parents as potential killers).

The young giant prefigures youth's assumptions of new kinds
of challenges (e.g., changing "the establishment" by overturning
its structures), the scorn inherent in young men's stances on
war, family, sex, and the durability of governments. The satire
deliberately overplays Victor's lucidity. Hyperbole is con-
torted; it grows out of proportion in its comic grotesqueness.
Victor the child dies. His innate savagery and wit can not compete, in the long run, with the world's sorry compromises.

The drama's historical strength was proven by a production
in 1962 and later ones in Paris. Flaws and anachronisms were
only minor obstacles. Less coherent, Vitrac's The Mysteries of
Love creates notable surrealist motifs and touches of effective-
ness as comedy. Foreseeing 1950-1970 savage plays (by Ionesco,
Genet, Arrabal), Vitrac sharpens our fascination with anthropomorphism (ox, snake, lobster, lamb, dog, goat are correlated to
human essences). Similarly, he evokes metamorphosis (phosphor-
us sleeps with Leah, a sparrow hawk is a dead person; characters
are all fishheaded; a mountain becomes a human being).

The old "romantic agony" veered in Vitrac's childhood-
oriented, rebellious hypotheses. The poet/playwright figure, no
longer a timorous, not-yet-in-full-bloom-individual, but a young

man reeling with indecision, now appears as self-assured. He has a barbed wit, masking his fear of insignificance. He castigates and blames parents behind a facade of bravado. No outward, Ubuesque monster, but an ominous heretic of early youth, Vitrac's hero plants seeds of social cataclysm and barbarism.

SEVEN: FIERCE DISSOLVENTS

LENORMAND

Nico, central character in H.-R. Lenormand's Time is a
Dream (1920), is no social seer, no aggressor. After a youth
of mystic ruminations in Java, Nico is sure that time has no
substance or certainty. Life is implausible. Man, disabused by
the categories he sets, does not move in time. His imaginative
realm is fraught with danger. Without the knowledge of time,
nothing can be analyzed with conviction. Dream sets its lures
inside us. Instincts of vitality dissolve, die. Love is one
of these; it is condemned to atrophy.

Climax of the play is discovery of Nico's suicide in a
misty pond. Contravening many of the usual precepts of psychology on stage, Nico indicates a portent. In theater, dark enigma
resurges. It is more than personal. Time and space start to
disconnect, no longer part of one continuum.

Critics jumped to a false conclusion. Lenormand was "illus-
trating" Einstein's theories of relativity. The playwright, on
the contrary, knew almost nothing of Einstein when he wrote Time
is a Dream. His play was inspired by adventures of friends who
had been in Java, primarily by the Dutch actress, Marie Kalff,
his future wife, and by the murky waters and landscapes in the
Netherlands. Not a philosopher, Lenormand (after 1923 a friend
of Eugene O'Neill) presaged French savage comedy of the 1930's
and 1940's. Fragmentation and dissolution of personality (Anouilh, Salacrou, Pinter, Mrozek, Beckett, Ionesco, Genet) were
stark in Time is a Dream.

Erroneously, commentators insisted that Lenormand was a
"disciple of Freud." At least three plays disprove the claim.
Man and his Phantoms (1924), The Dream Doctor (1922), and In
the Shadow of Evil (1924) are, if anything, anti-Freudian.

In an acrid drama with comic overtones, <u>Man and his Phan-</u>
<u>toms</u>, Lenormand sabotaged the reputed "omniscience" of Freudian
therapists. It was a new theme in theater. Untheoretical, the
play was founded on cases of women Lenormand had met in Swiss
asylums. Some of their treatments had been disastrous.

Roger, a Don Juan prototype, is a lone wolf, anti-tradi-
tional. He has had psychoanalysis. His feminine victims, expos-
ing his cruelties and weaknesses, rise up to haunt him in his
nightmarish delusions. Even while fully awake, Roger begins to
have terrors of death. Like virtually all Don Juans, in the
end, he dies, lacking full understanding of what he is. Part of
the cause of his death is mistaken therapy. His sexual anomaly
and other masquerades are unsolved.

<u>In the Shadow of Evil</u> shows Africa as a terrifying, psychic
dissolvent. The perverted Rougé, a colonial administrator, is
a mysterious symbol of evil. He is a metaphorical clue to Lenormand's prophecies about Africa and exotic "third-world" nations. Omens are double. The clash of European with "exotic"
cultures is on the way. This is a premonition in many of Lenormand's plays. Secondly, each of us has an "African" germ in his
instincts. Moral viciousness, unpredictability, and sudden
transformations of ethics (incarnate in African tropics) lurk in
every one. They merely await an impulse, a hair-fine trigger
which goes off without warning or rationality.

Lenormand, through Rougé, implies that moral savagery, pent
up, passionate to break its bonds, will choose its moment. No
one, perhaps, is exempt. (Wife-shoots-husband killings during
quarrels over trifles, a frequent, statistically huge pattern in
"civilized" countries, demonstrate this convincingly.) Religion, social taboos, and the strongest of atavisms are power-
less to halt the Rougés of our world. For they are obsessed,
misshapen by desire, inwardly unknowable. They are modern
savages. Rougé tortures natives without cause. He sees the

humanly-interpreted Cosmos as a net of willful evil, a concat-
ination of revenge piled upon revenge. His universe has no
place for good, only for the illusion of good. All is subter-
fuge. The irascible savage plays of 1930-1950, in virulence and
moral probing, were anticipated by Lenormand.

ARMAND SALACROU

Armand Salacrou, a Norman dramatist and wily businessman,
became favored by Parisian audiences as a "boulevard" playwright. He won more success on stage than Lenormand, whose
works rarely played in large theaters where fame was possible.
Salacrou's abrasive comedy-dramas reveal a brittle center. It
is a theme not unlike Pirandello's: We grasp our own paradoxes
too late. Do what we may, they tear our lives apart.

During a forty-year career (1920's to 1960's), Salacrou
shifted his drama perceptibly. First came a young man's surrealistic fancies (Poof, 1920; Circus Story, 1922), later hard-
bitten comedies and dramas (Histoire de Rire, 1939; L'Archipel
Lenoir, 1947; l'Inconnu d'Arras, 1935), and in full maturity,
Boulevard Durand, 1961.

Salacrou, as he evolved, revised the targets of his protagonists' revolts. Poof and Circus Story were enlivened by
Salacrou's zestful rebellion against theatrical conventional-
ities. In decor, language, and situation, the two comedies were
unusually effervescent. Rhythms broke. Characterizations melted, remnants flew into the air. Ideas bubbled and boiled, only
to explode. Movement was dashing, plot sparse, often unreal.

Salacrou's best-known style is his second phase: self-
ironizing disenchantment, gray in tone. Frequently somber in
metaphor, surprise-ending comedies were both ingenious and premonitory. In Histoire de Rire (Just for Laughs), two young
couples, both likeable, are thrown into a network of betrayal.
The play begins as a charming poetic comedy. Unexpectedly, it

rushes into sardonic, savage hypothesis. Death, the unsuspected shadow in the plot, takes form in a fierce denouement. A minor masterpiece, the play is a deeply-etched foreword to Ionesco's and Genet's dances of death.

Bitter and ludicrous social travesty, L'Archipel Lenoir features the cynical machinations devised by a Norman family when the old grandfather is accused of indecent advances to a woman less than half his age. A merry-go-round of immoral "solutions" is set in motion by schemers among the rich bourgeoisie. Salacrou, dramatic heir of France's pungent writers from Normandy (Flaubert, Maupassant), is ingenious and salty. His dialogue is juicy, at times rapacious; his denouements often amaze by savage-comedy deaths or reversals.

Boulevard Durand, inspired almost literally by a scandalous miscarriage of justice in Le Havre (where Salacrou had lived), is a scathing drama. The hero, Jules Durand, is condemned to die. He is accused of a unionist-management murder he did not commit. Vicious politics and problems of status rear ugly faces. They decide Durand's fate. Before he is to die, he is driven to insanity.

A drama of Salacrou's late maturity, Boulevard Durand has considerable power. Youthful dynamism has evolved into irony; the framework is unrelenting social vision and vengefulness. Before the public eye, Salacrou probes the sinkholes it would prefer not to see. As metaphor, Durand is also an omen of the future: victim of class callousness, the syndicalist sees all hope for change apparently killed.

JEAN ANOUILH

Famous for his craft, Jean Anouilh, one of France's leading artificers for the stage, seldom received his full due outside France. Translations slanted or diluted his plays. Anouilh trickily classified them in volumes as "rose," "black," "grating," "costumed," and so on. The labels are slippery.

Youth's longings betrayed and twisted into egotisms (a theme Salacrou had earlier intimated in depth) recur as an incessant motif throughout Anouilh's theater. His belligerent satires lament the pressures of our era (i.e., the inaccessibility of wealth, and its inescapable delusions, slicing into character).

Degradation is Anouilh's key. In his youthful comedies, The Savage and Thieves' Carnival, young protagonists fight against presages of their own personalities on the edges of corruption. Collective decadence and guilt are the culprits. Inward-turned, self-doubting, occasionally self-berating, Anouilh's plays are both rebellious and evanescent. Their comic folds, made of delusions within delusions, create a complex of mirrors. To extricate oneself is not easy. Anouilh's tantalizing theater was one of the most time-resistant of the period 1930-1970.

Anouilh described Thieves' Carnival (1932) as the cornerstone of his theater. In pristine suggestion, it includes almost all his major themes. A slight but magical comedy, Thieves' Carnival was conceived when Anouilh was in his early twenties. The comedy, ostensibly "rose" in optics, in fact pyramids metaphors of skepticism and resignation. The bases of existence are reflected as interconnected systems of thievery. Joined as images are the hypocrisies of social/financial status, time's maw as it gobbles up young destinies (life's potential is stolen before youth has a chance), love's bewilderments and ferocious inconstancies.

In the end, Love is the thief which misshapes all others. Its tentacles mangle while they steal. The fantasy's fleetingly conjectural, robber-aristocrat lovers (Gaston, Hector, Eva, Juliette, with Lady Hurf as ringmaster) flutter like finless goldfish, hemmed in by immovable walls, deprived, without sustenance. Love, in Anouilh's realms, is pretense, theatrical gamesmanship, desperate diversion and internal war, mysteriously waged on tracts of derisiveness. Impossibility reigns.

From the start, Thieves' Carnival plays to a musical motif. A clarinet, mocking and shrill, sounds Anouilh's life-defining disenchantment with the masked dynamics of what could be love. Anouilh had been impressed by Pirandello and Giraudoux. He sees time as a thief of life's latent artistries and all its potentials. Time is the ravaging corruptor. Our real selves are despoiled when status appears as tempter.

The aging Lady Hurf, who comments love's masquerades ironically in Thieves' Carnival, along with her rich cronies, brilliant caricatures of the toll of affluence on idealism, must keep concocting something to do. Or else life, fantasm for the wealthy, will stagnate, atrophy completely. Lady Hurf and Lord Edgard, her male counterpart, are near-phantoms. Their life-stultifying walls are money and dulled idleness.

When half-imaginary loves flicker for two young couples, they have no recourse but to theatricalize amorous illusions and desires. Thieves' Carnival finishes in this semi-terrestrial and fanciful register of poetry, where love is more dream than potentiality.

Anouilh's acidic comedies are top-heavy with the delusions of love. Some are feigned. Many defy time. All erode the self, which is blocked from probing and clarifying its hidden fabric, its authenticity. The crucial metaphor of life as tri-layered, theatricalized felony, which suffuses Thieves' Carnival, shaped Anouilh's lifelong imagery.

Traveler without Baggage (1936) is a harsh play. It is a zenith of savage comedy. Dark drama careens toward satire without ever attaining it. An anti-hero, Gaston, is an amnesiac. Rich matrons compete to claim him as a long-lost child. He becomes a cause célèbre. As Gaston confronts processions of would-be relatives, he little by little sniffs his own putrid past. Childhood reality and treachery, buried in amnesia, refuse to vanish. A sadistic crime against a boyhood friend climaxes these other-world horrors.

Gaston senses family ties broken by his lust, hatred, and ingratitude. In Anouilh's unsavory characterization of the anti-hero filter some of the playwright's most acrid views of youth. Distrust, not affection, rules families. Brother attacks brother in adulterous vengeance. A child brutally maims his friend.

Traveler without Baggage, a backward-peering dramatic parable, intensifies comic astringency and fierceness. Rapacity strikes inward; seeing himself as monstrous, Gaston cleverly renounces his past and "escapes" it. The play's black-comic strength lies in Gaston's half-repentant savagery, as it obeys instincts for preservation. This overrides the play's deus-ex-machina ending, which purports to wipe his life clean.

In the threads which united to give form to savage comedy, Anouilh's The Savage (1934) is central. It is an ironically split portrait. Thérèse, the heroine, squirms in a nest of social vipers. She is at once fascinated and repelled by the wealth of a virtuoso pianist, Florent. Her queasy hesitations, pushing her close to self-doubling, are The Savage's basic leit-motifs.

"Savage" because she fights to stay untamed and uncorrupted, Thérèse in the end spurns Florent and his riches. Her metaphorical "No!" is crucial in Anouilh's dramatic thought. As a young, penniless author, he was infuriated by the callousness of success formulae. In revolt, he interpreted existence as self-degrading capitulation to all the forces and effects of money. Thérèse's savagery (beyond its romantic individualism) is mockery of the erosion of will which eats at affluence with the slow decay of judgment money enforces.

The Savage is a notable savage comedy. Anouilh's satiric acid finds marks in the posturing pseudo-actors and musicians who engulf Thérèse. In irony's decay, Thérèse does not escape.

Divisiveness in the heroine's personality gives The Savage a razor edge. The play, a prototype for many others in Anouilh's opus, is one of his most rasping visions.

A grotesque replica of "normal" love bringing together two ill-fated hunchbacks incites the action in Ardèle ou la Marguerite (1948). The deformed couple's passion is fatal. Counterpointed to this destiny are respectability's inane affairs of the flesh, which go on, half-alive. Each of these is a masquerade of sincerity. Behind masks are cynical, animal-like lusts. One by one, each slumps.

Socially esteemed, cynical lovers—as Anouilh's savage comedies frequently show—find ways to smash non-conformists, who are defenseless, involuntarily estranged from society. Ardèle and her love, whose guilt is that of being misshapen, abandon life, which is dictated by the piously cruel. Ardèle has moments of overdone pathos. All the same, it is one of Anouilh's shattering dark comedies. The pre-destined hunchbacks, savage despite themselves, refuse to fade from our memories. Ardèle's uniqueness grows from a hyperbole: "sane" and "twisted" loves, unable to realize and live their special natures (either as hunchbacks or as accepted shapes) seethe with permanent disquiet. This is Anouilh's irony, his near-genius in savage dramatization.

Ferocities sharpen title and theatrical poignance in Colombe (1951). In a French province, a cloistered entertainment milieu turns a dove-like young woman into an alluring, star actress. Colombe, at first a submissive wife, suddenly is a self-contradiction: a captious, resourceful and seductive actress.

Lucien, Colombe's husband, trails through his worm's routines, harassed by doubt, jealousy, hesitation, recoil. Unusually telling is Anouilh's skill in juxtaposing male and female fears of futures which teeter in the balance. Lucien and Colombe juggle timorously with love's feints and reprisals. Fantasy overturns; it spins dizzily, producing bitter twists. These are semi-comic, semi-fearful. Colombe insinuates a ferocious conclusion: love feeds on distress, but it can also choke on it. An identical paradox was to be rephrased by Ionesco (<u>Exit the King</u>, <u>The Bald Soprano</u>), Genet, and Arrabal. It is a core of savage comedy.

Queasily, the comic individualist (playwright or his character), doubtful in his marrow about beliefs in his "Cosmos wrenched out of its tracks," is forced to try new angles. The known ones pall. At times his angular biases, his search, bring him into monstrosities or modern fables unpalatable to most. Hunchbacks, born <u>in</u> this world, are not born <u>for</u> this world. An automatism of the twentieth-century seems to decree: hunchbacks are to be erased. The sight of them does not fit. They do not belong. Love is not for them. On a plane of respectability, a glamorous woman can not reconcile the two-sidedness of virtuous wife and actress. A savage protagonist, split, can not reject riches with impunity. Punishment must come. One's vicious past sticks like paint; it has to be carried, ineradicable, as life's required baggage; even the ruthlessness of childhood will be unmasked one day; it is a part of us, clinging, ever-present.

Anouilh's crucial savage-comedy metaphor involves self-wounding backlash when a resister furiously counterattacks social fakery and cowardice. It recurs throughout his plays, almost inexhaustible, like a haunted phrase of music.

EIGHT: DREAD TURNS COMIC: (A NEW GENERATION)

About a generation later, Ionesco (<u>Rhinoceros</u>, <u>Amédée</u>, <u>The Lesson</u>), Genet (<u>The Maids</u>, <u>The Balcony</u>) and Arrabal (<u>The Architect and the Emperor of Abyssinia</u>) set free wild new figures of animalesque humanoids. They served to repeople the social menageries and the ommegang march of <u>grotesqueries</u> caricatured by Anouilh, Vitrac, and Lenormand.

In Ionesco's <u>Rhinoceros</u> (1959), the symbol of humans-become-horned beasts clearly announced the processes of dehumanization. In other plays, Ionesco's nightmares of feet engulfing a room, chairs squeezing an old couple closer to death, languages on the point of cosmic explosion, corpses invading life, are visions of a threatened and threatening universe, out of man's control. As a boy, Ionesco learned that Storm Troopers of World War II were capturing his neighbors in Rumania. Many did not return. Fear of death, Ionesco admitted, was always his primary impulse as playwright. His ominous imagery of proliferation, explosions, time's onslaughts, and even linguistic inertness spring from this sense of mortal peril.

Genet's <u>The Balcony</u> (1960) delves into social-sexual fantasmagoria. These crystallize to take shape as unforeseen (though poetically credible) metamorphoses. A judge melts. He turns into victim and lost soul. From sadist, he mutates to weakling. Born of the oneiric action in a bordello, illusion and reality clang, shock, then mingle. Outside the house, a revolution forces near-union of real and illusory. Stunning reversals of character and metaphor are Genet's devices in a stiletto-edged, quasi-Pirandellian nightmare comedy.

Anouilh's revolts, whether psychic or moral, are embodied typically in amorous, political, or obliquely military caricature. <u>The Waltz of the Toreadors</u> (1952) features two ludicrous facsimiles of love. Both portray General Saint-Pé, one of

Anouilh's favorite, reappearing anti-heros. Retired from warfare but still nostalgically sidling up to an old flame, the
general is tied in a knot by his supposedly moribund but vixen-
ish wife and his mistress, a maidservant.

The general's devilish little son seeks a second generation's vengeance. He apes his father's dallying, as he tries
to waylay girls his age or older. The boy, a prototype of frus-
trated, precocious vengefulness in Anouilh's theater, transmits
the omens Roger Vitrac had splashed on stage in Victor ou les
Enfants au Pouvoir: adults are despoilers; they bring havoc to
family, false instruction to children, and inane concepts which
typify national and international foresight. Anouilh's plays
incessantly lead to a main part of twentieth-century Angst: the
despair of plundered innocence, unregainable.

The Waltz of the Toreadors, burlesque in externals, is an
effort to reshape time's irreversible past-to-present cyclic
charade. It is a half-laughable revelation of the general's
erotic boiling at an advanced age. His youthful fires refuse to
subside. Domesticity and its servitudes also have him trapped.

During amorous outbursts, General Saint-Pé pinpoints Anouilh's focus on the wreckage of matrimony. The state of co-exis-
tence saps a rebel's vigor. Thus the embattled (though derisory) fighter is robbed of his potential nuances, his hidden
self. Before they can be plumbed, depths block.

Existence is like a grimy steamroller. Unstoppable, it
flattens humps and deviations. It deflates the joie de vivre
of all Saint-Pés. Yet in barbarous stubbornness, they still
cling to outcropping boulders as destruction approaches.

Poor Bitos (1956) is a pugnacious satire. Anouilh's mature
imagery gives it notable stridency. Its comedy is savage, whiplash. Twin optics interpret Bitos. He is both hero and target
of derision. The play, not widely performed outside France, is
redoubtable. Its structure in figurative layers and its allu-
sions are not easy to follow.

Once an impoverished student, Bitos is now a jurist. Old comrades invite him to a masked dinner. The others force him to disguise as Robespierre. At the banquet, scurrilous gibe, insult, and counter-insult swarm around Bitos-Robespierre. Historical barbarism connected with the French Revolution's aftermaths of terror merges with play-acted man versus adversary. Crescendos accentuate multiple-focus battles of personality, hatreds, and blood lust.

The real Bitos, freed from his Robespierre persona, evades death at the hands of his adversaries. In mental disarray, he escapes. Curiously, Bitos is emboldened by what seem to be adverse glimmers of his life and secret being.

Poor Bitos is murky, at least in parts. Yet it intensifies two savage comedy outlooks: (1) The self-isolated character will be snagged on the warp which twists existence in an inexorably-structured society. He reacts with intransigeant, sometimes brutish ferocity. (2) If a rebel accepts the societal web, it will be deleterious, possibly murderous.

Shortly after Anouilh's Poor Bitos and its Pirandellian maze of fierceness and betrayal, theater began to portray new types of antimonies and antagonisms in Europe and in the United States. Edward Albee's pungent, imagistic battlers, George and Martha, who combat history and the future in Who's Afraid of Virginia Woolf? (1962) or Pinter's subversive, disintegrating family units (The Homecoming, 1965), typify new and upsetting sorts of savage comedy. A modern combat becomes describable: "The Lone Savage," in part imponderable, wars against "The Encroaching Web," society's ironclad concepts.

Shakespeare, as Robert Hatch observed, "did not mix absurdity with terror or hilarity with disgust."[1] After 1950, certain French playwrights instinctively stirred these unstable ingredients together. The mixtures produced theatrical explosions. Recipes varied. Ionesco, as we have seen, declared that dread of dying was the matrix for his plays. Beckett's dramas were given special pulsation by death's not-too-distant-hand, poised somewhere close. Genet aimed to sabotage bourgeois indoctrination's wellsprings. He sharpened the stimuli of daydream so as to pierce life's hypocritical filth and make it spill out. On stage, Genet meant to alchemize the dross of vice and crime into silver, via the poetic brews of language. He used sleight-of-hand, magic verbal and visual transmutations.

More outlandish still were Fernando Arrabal's savagely obscene, grotesque plays. On the most obvious level of plot, juvenile or buffoonish, an Arrabal play recalls the cruelties of childhood, its vicious curiosities and desires. Underneath, in lairs of revery, Arrabal concocts a rare species of luxuriance, interweaving childlikeness and adolescence with fragments of adulthood.

About 1950, some of the avant-garde plays in France and other European countries, then England and the United States, began to be categorized by newly-invented terms. "Absurd theater" was the most durable. First proposed by Martin Esslin, who adapted Camus's concept, it won wide acceptance. Others were less frequently used: metaphysical farce, anti-theater, tragic farce, tragicomedy, existential farce, metatheater, and so on. None proved to be an ideal description.

Savage comedy, while not a genre, is distinguished by its outlook and its metaphorical unity. It is a mode or tone of modern theater. On derisory planes, it dramatizes rapacity, individual and collective. Ripostes come from rebellious misfits. A pseudo-Hamletic, unsettled Cosmos is implied. Paradoxically, the clash of extremes may elicit laughter. Life-views hinted in a hero or heroine, not always easy to discern, are critical. A central figure, both barbarous and recoiling, struggles to break through the thickets of a more or less impenetrable milieu. If he does, he can begin to create his foreseeable becoming.

Not cruelty _per se_, but inward-cramping frustration, aggravated by anti-societal phobias and terrors, ties a protagonist, who remains recalcitrant.

The savage comedy hero does not see his environment and its ravages as fixed. Nor does he deem them philosophically absurd or inconsequential. He meets, everywhere he goes, acts analogous to those committed by rapacious brutes. His enemy appears to be the flaw in his Cosmos, murderous, falsifying, greedy, hostile to his very essence. But metamorphosis is their law. They are not predictable. Nor is he. Form changes, mutations are rife.

NINE: MASTERWORKS

IONESCO

The Bald Soprano (1950) by Ionesco ricochets zany, unworldly speech and puzzling inaction in half-crazy pace. Vertigo arises and lingers, quite unforgettable. Fast-sprouting metamorphoses shoot out and burst. Two British couples, the Smiths and the Martins, redistill cliché-language, in the end inventing and poetizing its wildest fragments. World of the nonsensical, giddy non sequiturs, gibberish, and upside-down metaphorical fantasies make this mix palatable inside the frame of ferocious, parodied comedy. Laws governing dramatic progression, identity, and logic are shattered or badly bruised.

What is The Bald Soprano's enduring savage-comic hypnotics? Ionesco, while seeming to make fun of decadent and grotesque sterility of chatter in a middle-class British home, actually prophesies something vaster. The satire foretells the zero-approaching inanity which eats away human relationships. Almost every character in The Bald Soprano loses logical outline. In the process, he risks tumbling into nonentity, or even into some else's skin. Ionesco's implied terror at individuality's decay is rampant in the comic metaphors. Wrapped in cloaks of fancy, this figurative erosion cavorts fearfully with language on a rampage. (Rhinoceros is impelled by a parallel motif.)

Ionesco's maid and fireman, even his British clock behave with a kind of metallic and brittle anti-logic. Grotesquerie, here, is laughable, once the splintering, sharp-tongue-in-cheek parody of vitality and theatrical animus deepens. We watch logically clear absolutes explode. The inane appears to win a war of styles. Ionesco balances dizzy dramatic data. When old language has breathed its last, unearthly artifacts and reshapings exert mysterious power on stage. When identity has faded away, its definitions gone, an audience may begin to accept comic metamorphoses. Smiths become Martins, and vice-versa. The comedy's conclusion produces the same comedy's beginning. With Ionesco, theatrical esthetics have performed a double-backward flip, with no hands.

During and since Wrold War II, human beings have apparently suffered from lessened resistance to forces that have "lathe-turned" them into conscienceless brutes. This was one of Ionesco's pervasive dreads. It underlies many of his savage comedies. Rhinoceros exudes this fear. In a French village, everyone except the lazy, unheroic Bérenger willingly mutates into a rhino. The others all want to be one of the herd. "It's what every one's doing," the conformist's rationale, and "If I don't follow I'm afraid of the consequences," the coward's confession, are capsular parables of soft-minded capitulations to Nazi tyranny. They also foreshadow present-day crushers of mentality: newspapers, big-money interests, politics, TV, family, nation.

The Lesson (1951) is a ferociously onrushing nightmare. It is an eerie comedy bathed in the gruesome. In fantasmagoria, the "semi-sophisticated brute" attains mortal impact. The "lesson," unlike any ever given in a civilized salon, begins in approximate normalcy. An erudite professor and his student, a young woman, banter inept ideas on "world philology." After a paroxysm in unintelligible words, both funny and frightening, the professor's oratory races out of control into authoritarian gobbledygook. The student's toothache (symbol of erotic terror) metamorphoses her into a provocative, junior harpie. This transformation, counterpointed by the professor's fantasies, brings about her death. Sexual violation and murder (continuing a long series the professor has committed) end a shocking parody of discovery. Though cruel and ghastly if viewed literally, The Lesson stimulates uneasy laughter. Dread of death and violation, transmuted by Ionesco's frenetic, anti-logical style, are purged through comedy. Dread is now comic.

The Lesson is an apex of savage theater. Its tones mutate into semi-surrealistic disconnectedness. Ionesco disarticulates language, gesture, psychology, reason--and above all, dramatic symbol. Splinters fly; only a few rejoin their origins.

Ionesco's first plays are crucial. In each, he extravagantly depicts "automatisms" by unbelievable travesty, so as to insinuate sub-human behavior. The Lesson features hyperbolic grotesquerie in the medium of imagined languages not simply for the shock effects. The play broaches a new technique of satire.

Automaton-teachers (and perhaps sadistic, lustful adventurers) are legion. So are puzzled and inept students. In The Lesson's cascading mental pace, which projects the girl into murder, Ionesco's satiric jabs avoid absolutes. They compel attention. The professor's dictatorial obsession is the belief that all languages join philologically. It is his "logic" as well as the comedy's anti-logic. Metaphor of intellectual repression, it transforms itself in the end. Now tyranny is unmistakeable. The professor forces the girl to accept his theories. She has no choice. Totalitarian cruelty, her naive capitulation, her toothache raging worse and worse, then the final assault and killing are like figurative ladders stretching into tyranny and total submission. The tone is that of agony.

The professor, no savage semi-hero like Bérenger, is nearly surreal. He represents the brutishness of intellectual single-mindedness run wild. He comes from a weirdly metaphorical, middle-class society unable to see dictatorship in official high collars. Nor is his victim a heroine or martyr. Too dull to tell language from non-language, teacher from non-teacher, she speeds disaster.

As Jarry had done in King Ubu, Ionesco insidiously sculpts comic hyperbole to the heights of savagery. In so doing, he effaces standard criteria for verisimilitude. Ionesco hints at notions of non-professor as a grotesque extreme, as some species

of other-worldly pedagogue. But the ultimate links in our vision
of the professor-concept are not torn away. Our inner under-
standings of a manic teacher extend, wider and deeper.

Why are savage comedy playwrights obsessed by human involve-
ments in certain kinds of metamorphosis? Theology has pointed to
possible answers. The "God is Dead" theologians of the 1950's
and 1960's, tardily adapting Nietzsche's postulates and influ-
enced by Camus's pagan scepticism, phrased a telling suspicion.
Divine certainty may prove to be unintelligible; if so, divine
plan in intangible.

When faith in divine absolutes is explicitly or implicitly
corroded, human character may have to be slowly transformed, in
ways parallel to those seen in nature's evolutions. This may
happen despite divine or cosmic structural systems.

Surrealism (especially in poetry and theater) was fecund in
imagery tinted with animism and pantheism, as well as innumer-
able irreligious and cosmic analogies. God-as-all-knowing, God
as solace for broken loves (à la Hugo or Lamartine) was seldom
found in the poetic mainstream in France after Apollinaire and
1916.

Even more than poetry, experimental drama edged closer to
revery embodied half-logically, to up-dated myth, nightmare,
sustained fantasy, and "directed dream."

There were belligerent ideas of having escaped from God's
order, if not all the orderliness of divinity. Religious inhib-
itions faded. On stage, forms of existence, habits, and aims
shifted faster than ever before. In dream-impregnated plays,
man visualized himself in new guises, with transfigured possibilities. Genet (The Balcony, The Maids), Ionesco (Rhinoceros and
elsewhere) and Arrabal created bedazzled oneiric scenes to convey
human transformations.

Amédée, ou Comment s'en débarrasser (1954, Amédée, or How
to get rid of it) reflected Ionesco's obsession with superabun-
dance of things and the fearfulness this causes. Amédée is unable

to slow the vertiginous growth of feet which menace his vital space. These expanding feet seem ready to invade his being. Ionesco's anti-hero, Amédée, is a picture of post-atomic man trampled by the speed and ruthlessness of technological acceleration. Other dangers will soon surround him: automobiles (larger and more deadly than fierce animals), computers reproducing themselves more rapidly than wildfire to track every citizen inside his secret vices.

In Rhinoceros (1960), which won epochal success in Germany before it opened in Paris, a memorable image is that of abrupt human metamorphosis. A paradox casts Ionesco's resister, Bérenger, as an indolent, cafe-lounging, unambitious bureaucrat. When his friend Jean, mouthing platitudes of civic virtue, acquiesces to mob psychology and turns into a rhinoceros, Bérenger has a salutary shock. He refuses mutation, declining to be a rhino.

Besides being a quizzical metaphor of the little man's anti-fascist revolt, Bérenger incarnates more. Proclaiming his intention to remain the last and only one of his species, whatever the cost, he rejects the most overpowering truism of the epoch: "Others are all doing it now, why not me?" Bérenger, a strange brand of non-conformist and resister, means to conserve at any cost the exact nature his human breed has evolved. With it, he will guard his identity and potential. One senses that Bérenger will repulse the lures of any fiercer hordes, of whatever nature. The prophecy is clear.

Metamorphosed ex-human beings have followed leaders in rhinoceritis, happy not to face harder decisions. Bérenger, though he is initially a-heroic, emerges as if from a void, finds and activates savage comedy's dynamics in the last act. Atavisms buried within him rise. Bérenger fights to stay what he is, flaws and all, to sustain his species.

Rhinoceros is a stampede of human transmutations. If watched on the surfaces of visual comedy, these are hilarious. Savage theater's enigmas lurk below. In early scenes of Rhinoc-

eros, Bérenger is a loafer, unthinking. Despite his inauspicious
beginnings, he somehow gains fortitude. Aghast, he sees his
friend Jean change into a rhino. This is the determining blow.
All by himself he becomes a resister, against thought control.
Out of near-nothingness comes the heroism of revolt. The comic-
serious hyperbole is memorable. For we believe. Comedy's savagery, weighted into the starkness of near-to-life drama, enables
our minds to understand a parable of brainwashing. Seen in its
entirety, however, Rhinoceros is not characterized by savage
comedy tonalities.

Exit the King (1962) and L'Epidémie ou Jeux de Massacre
(1970) ressuscitate the primary ghost of Ionesco's career: fear
of dying. In 1954, the playwright told obliquely of this terror,
linking it to his obsessions with evanescence and weight:

> "Two fundamental states of consciousness are at the
> origin of all my plays...that of evanescence and of weight;
> of the void and of excess presence; of the unreal trans-
> parency of the world and of its opacity; of light and of
> thick darkness."[1]

Ionesco had written more concretely in 1934 of death's grip
on his obsessions:

> "I am afraid of death. I am afraid to die, no doubt
> because, without knowing it, I want to die. So I am afraid
> of the desire I have to die."[2]

To an interviewer, Claude Bonnefoy, Ionesco asserted that
Exit the King was "an apprentice's try at death."[3] Not society,
but death is the antagonist of King Bérenger the First, lyric/
savage protagonist of Exit the King. The king's relentless
revolt against the imminence of death, all his refusals to let
go of life and its scant pleasures, are intended to ward off the
ominous figure coming closer with the sickle.

King Bérenger (who has brushed aside his mortality for centuries) is a quizzical savage comedy hero. The play is a eulogy
to life's tiny instants of joy, not mainly a comedy or a dirge.
Marie, the king's second wife, relates the raptures of just being
alive. Listening, Bérenger senses that his long past as monarch

and lover still demonstrates the vitality he yearns to reassume. The king, silly, at times odious, lucid though self-centered, is an acutely-drawn figure of royalty. As Claude Abastado saw, "...he is Man...nest of desires and anguish." By his every stratagem, King Bérenger is a striking metaphor for all those who seek to outmanoeuver Death.

L'Epidémie ou Jeux de Massacre is transmuted into a peripheral savage comedy by means of an incomplete voice. The voice is implicit. It is the one we can almost hear, coming from a semi-overt Ionesco. The playwright again addresses himself to Death, supreme adversary, ubiquitous.

L'Epidémie was partly inspired by DeFoe's Diary of a Plague and Camus's The Plague. It is a hair-raising multiplication of deaths strewn as though willy-nilly by a pestilence, mysterious in origin. Comic and pitiful effects are highlighted when the dying and the threatened bare their secret foibles. These range from arrogance to evaporating tenderness, hope, inanity, cruelty, terror, abrupt compassion. When the plague ends, half the populace dead, a huge fire erupts.

As always, Ionesco's dilemmas are stark and insoluble. Why Death's depredations en masse? Why its spasms, its arbitrary wars, which seem to be cyclical, forcing man to slaughter man? Is Death itself a mechanism racing beyond any control? If so, Ionesco's implicit, savage-comic lament is doubly meaningful: "I disobey; I refuse to capitulate to a Cosmos in disarray."

Ionesco challenges a grinding, almost certainly bellicose Cosmos. Less categorical than Dürrenmatt (whose visions of interplanetary chaos and "monstrosity" are central) Ionesco revives childhood terrors (Nazi storm troopers, disappearances increasing dizzyingly, moral surrenders under political pressure, mortality's omnipresence) to write savage comedies. These invented an anti-toxic, new language for theater. Metamorphoses signaled outlandish foresights. Ionesco traced non-psychical stage personae, unlike those of any predecessor. He shredded psychology, to build metaphorical labyrinths without exits.

GENET

Jean Genet's plays are permeated by fantasy's role-changing, seemingly impermanent metamorphoses. Poet of class and race antagonism, Genet has now and then been interpreted as a modern Villon with a social mission. He is denunciatory and quasi-Satanic. As playwright, Genet unleashes nether forces to have them feast on twentieth-century man's entrails. His maids, madams, revolutionaries, Arabs and ethnic rebels often seem to be transfigured by revery, revenge, and transitory illusion. Some claim to assume new guises, perhaps those of "respectable" alter egos. Genet's paradox damns them to illusionism: "sincerity" is falsehood, sexual anomaly, inversions of ethnicity, poison.

The Maids (1947), The Balcony (1956) and The Blacks (1958) vivify Genet's nightmare realm. His characters, anti-realistic, are figurative signs which pulsate. They combine in eerie theatrical tropes of reacting and unexplained becoming. They are uniquely terror-fraught. Above all, they are designed to baffle and pierce the imagination deeply, so that lucidity may seep out.

Contempt is a deathly virus. The Maids is founded on this aphorism. In this savage drama, which contains little comedy, the virus as perversely social metaphor is visible in a number of shapes. Its implications are complex. The two maids, Claire ("clear") and Solange ("sun/angel") slip into death-inviting transfigurations. In morbid rituals, they feign "being" Madame, their employer (in fact, an almost-bourgeoise whore). They also ritualize purified versions of their own egos. Finally, Solange offers Claire poisoned tea which had been destined for Madame. Envy and hatred of richer classes, combining with self-scorn, prove fatal as metamorphosing distillates.

The Balcony, Genet's scandalous, richly-patterned bordello

play, has comic aspects. It draws power not from single-imaged eroticism but from its careening, symbolic structure/upon/structure of sensual powers. As Kenneth Tynan noted, Genet envisions characters enslaved by the symbols of power, trapped in magnetic erotics: "The image of power is erotic; but power itself is sexless. The reality survives by enslaving man to the symbol."[4]

Habitués of the brothel, chasing elusive fantasies, disguise. When a revolution exterminates nearly all the power-elite, travestied clients perform their desired new identities: General, Judge, Monarch, Bishop, warrior. A self-constituted "Chief of Police" castrates himself. Genet's imagistic hints are scathing. Prestige does not confer heightened moral or sexual vigor. The top leaders in a society may lose their potencies.

In both The Balcony and The Maids, savage comedies heard black laughter arise. Stifled quickly by images of lusts seldom admitted, each was endowed with bizarre dimensions. Fierce (though poetized) echos of the century's inadmissable repressions penetrate, purposefully dissonant. They are Genet's forte. A modern barbarian in theme and lyrical clash, he links convict and déclassé and pins psychological rebels in scabrous culs-de-sac, ego-dilemmas.

The Blacks (1958), in murderous ceremonies, transpose the most ravenous desires that haunt blacks' intricate self-images. Primary is venomous hatred of the whites. Queasiness runs through the play's structure, which—hard to decipher in totality—is created by seething layers of ritual within ritual. Plot (the equivocal murder of a white woman) flickers, fleeting and enigmatic. Uncertainty thickens, instead of moving toward transparence.

The tone of The Blacks is vibrant corrosiveness, resistance. Symbol surmounts, displaces, transmutes other symbol. Basic is the ritualized murder and its obliteration of the enemy's tyranny. Revery sings about destruction of white mastery. Genet, who champions revolts by oppressed underdogs, reaches an apex of his

urgency in <u>The Blacks</u>. The play's savagery calls forth little
laughter. Only in the deepest senses are Genet's plays comic.
Ludicrous, vengeful man sees himself. His bizarre frustrations,
hidden under crusts of pretense, are derisory, when made into
scenic metaphor.

Barbarous, nether-world mirrors of evil and caricature make
Genet's theater glitter with conjurations. How can comic reactions greet Genet's revolutionary plays? From spectator to spectator, the answer varies deeply. <u>The Balcony</u>, Genet's most lush
theatrical dream, has a structure of convoluted fantasm. Satire
is strong in inversions of Eros. These make the spectator recognize his ridiculous sexual and power-grabbing impulses. <u>The
Blacks</u> is denser. Moral travesty and Luciferian games of disguised hatreds, even death as a travesty, murder as mode of
feeling and concept: few invite laughter overtly. Genet's
extraordinary gifts, pitch-black comic, are preponderantly
acidic. His games with identity and social critique, not unlike
some of Pirandello's, rattle our bones of derisiveness with inadmissable truths. Underneath, a criminal's daydreaming of revolt
knits disparity into irony.

ARRABAL

Fernando Arrabal, Spanish émigré and anti-Franco writer,
took refuge in Paris. There he conceived his astounding and
unearthly plays. Among his productions, some pandered to eroticism. Others used blasphemy. They came close to eliminating
linearity of traditional kinds. Elsewhere, Arrabal joined a multiplicity of these ingredients by means of fierce innovations.
Prolific, sometimes shockingly uneven in his talents, Arrabal
became the most controversial poet of the French theater since
the famous trio of Genet, Beckett, and Ionesco.

Arrabal's plays, with a few exceptions, defy clearcut clas-
sification. Neither comedy nor tragedy, drama nor farce, melo-

74

drama nor political satire, they seem to waver, as if in search of some safe theatrical limbo. Arrabal coined the term "Panic Play" for one phase of his works. (He admitted that he wanted to evoke "Pan," or "All.") The dramatist described his Panic plays as "a theater where humor, and poetry, panic and love would all be one...Profusion and austerity combine."[5]

How was "the comic" separable, by 1950-1960, from what had been considered "tragic"? In Discovering the Theatre (p. 86), Ionesco pinpointed an adverse modern reaction to the classic concepts of comic and tragic: "the comical is tragic and the tragedy of man derisory." A wrenched hyperbole, it would seem. But if we admit this claim, in any degree, the comedy of ferocious impulses is logically inevitable; it is a necessity.

Arrabal splits drama and comedy into wild love/hate teeterings. He twists "grave comedy" and metaphysical farce, using, as it were, bold injections of adrenalin to revive semi-moribund patients. In Arrabal's plays, literal savagery is a vision straight from nightmare. It may be central in thematics; or it may be evoked on action's fringes.

Fando et Lis (1958) is characteristic of Arrabal's first manner. On the way to Tar (nowhere), Fando pushes the paralyzed Lis in a wheelchair. Though he loves her, he exposes her bodily to other men. Overnight, he bares her to the elements. In pathological, hateful love frenzy, Fando beats and kills Lis. With a dog and a flower, he visits her grave, fulfilling a promise he had made to his victim.

As waifs lost forever who see each other in a tormented fairy story, Fando and Lis form the matrix for countless obsession-haunted, youthful Arrabal couples. The playwright telescopes an adult lifetime, as children might imagine it. Rapacious, killing instincts spurt out.

Life is wiped out senselessly. The play's fabric is colored by ambivalences, usually irreducible (love-hatred, purity-perversity, hope-disbelief). The savage comedy lurches like a sardonic

mechanism toward death. <u>Fando and Lis</u>, with its capricious torture and murder, prefigured the cult of brutality for brutality's
sake which pervaded Western theater and film after 1965.

Freud, among other psychologists, has illuminated the rapa-
ciously split drives of hateful love. The theme is as ancient
as literature. In Arrabal's theater, it goes on a rampage. The
dramatist claimed that his plays were rooted in his recurrent
dreams, which led him compulsively to awakened fantasms. Arrabal's paternal fixation (his own father inexplicably disappeared
in Spain) and an amalgam of suspicious love for his mother were
crucial in the playwright's obsessions.

The hero of <u>The Automobile Graveyard</u> (1958) is Emanou, jazz
trumpetist (Emmanuel), a blasphemous Christ figure. He lives in
an orgiastic automobile junkyard. Christ's passion is grotesquely
metamorphosed through Emmanuel and the prostitute Dila, two police
informers and a musical combo which plays for nightly dancing.
Dila's favors are available without restriction.

By a kiss, a clarinetist, Topo, betrays Emanou to the
police. After undergoing a vicious beating, the Christ-hero,
arms bound and widespread, his body cross-shaped on bicycle han-
dlebars, is in death throes. Junkyard orgies, unaffected, go
ahead.

Arrabal's pathological hatred of police (a vestige of childhood in Franco's Spain), warps <u>The Automobile Graveyard</u>. Naive
longing for love, unusual in intensity, and desire to regain
childlikeness (a generative base of Arrabal's theater) are splintered by police repression. Persecution seems barbaric. Human
menaces and death lurk. In Arrabal's universe, ongoing tenderness or charity must be delusions. As central threads of human
nature, they fritter away, apparently worn out.

Police-state pathology was a shaping element in Arrabal's
theater. Entropy of faith in the individual, shown as twisted
and pulverized, induces a careening toward panic. Fear is a
norm. Fear of what? A play, seen as a unit, may obscure this.

76

Some omnipotent, savagely impersonal menace waits in Arrabal's cracked Cosmos, ready at any time to snuff out a rebellious dreamer's chances to be himself.

A link comes to view. It seems to unify the images of governmental tyranny and the punishing arbitrariness of the post-atomic universe. Yet this is not certain. It is Arrabal's riddle. This cosmic puzzle and man's repression combine in The Automobile Graveyard to provoke murder. The enigma is, by any ordinary standards, well-nigh inscrutable.

A natural order is perpetuated when police kill Emanou. Metaphorical rapacity and actual slaughter merge. A universe is stripped of metaphysical explanation. Its beginnings, its processes, are dark. Persecution oozes from it. Insidiously, this theatrical Cosmos shrieks what humanity is and is becoming. Grotesquely misshapen self-torture and personality's irremediable self-twisting, are metaphors we would prefer to flee but can not.

Fando and Lis pivots on one shocking act. It might be called "defensive murder." Fando kills Lis, perhaps in subconscious dread. He removes her from an existence devoid of hope for achievement. Nor can she expect permanent tenderness or understanding. Arrabal's realms show no confidence in such chimera. His plays are spotted with similar killings and tortures.

Arrabal's "Panic Theater" (1965-67) swerved abruptly away from the naive visions of his first style. With slight overstatement, Martin Esslin described the latter group as veritable black masses of the stage.[6] Le Couronnement (1965) and Le Grand Cérémonial (1966) are intricate in gradations of plot and analogy. Overall, they depend unduly on sensationalism and on cruel erotic titillations. Not many spectators are likely to be convinced.

The Architect and the Emperor of Assyria (1967) swirls and plunges deeper. It is one of Arrabal's most lurid plays. Controversy is its purpose. The savage comedy's long-running success in Paris was Arrabal's stepping stone to celebrity.

Physical metamorphosis is the crux of the imagistic and
ludicrous plot. The Emperor, torrentially verbose, an egomaniac
travesty of intellectualism lost on a self-modelled dream site,
tries to sophisticate the Architect. They are in fact on a for-
lorn island. The two oneiric characters go through outlandish
transformations. Some of these are merely mimed. Others are
eancted bodily. Transvestive shifts unfold. So does cannibalism.
Arrabal's wild genius in stage pyrotechnics and grotesqueries
rescue the play from ego-flaunting.

The barbaric, torture-inflicting Cosmos Arrabal creates for
the theater centers in his ego, extraordinarily unsettled. Arrabal's world revolves or interchanges two prototypes (the Fando/
Lis couple-matrix). At times the two switch sexes. A mature
adaptation is that of the Emperor and the Architect, who compulsively metamorphose and cannibalize on an island given form by
revery. These two reverse sex, then identities themselves.
Though men in name, they are really recastings, in prophetic
metaphor (also shaped from torture and suffering), of Arrabal's
unquenchable nightmares of a police-state world coming to being.

BECKETT   (THE ASSASSINATION OF TIME)

King Ubu's murderous clowneries in 1896 hypothesized omens
that Rimbaud's pre-announced "time of assassins" might be
approaching. When hundreds of thousands were slain in World
War I and countless numbers twenty to thirty years later in
Stalin's and Hitler's pogroms and purges, the Viet-Nam war came
after another generation, and bloodlettings opposed adversaries
in dozens of nations, small or immense, Ubu's carnage lived in
the blood of history.

In 1953, with Waiting for Godot, Samuel Beckett won
eminence as playwright. Just eight years earlier, American
atomic bombs had pulverized, then sickened Hiroshima and Naga-
saki. The post-atomic epoch was at hand. Many European con-

sciences reacted vehemently to the atrocities produced by atomic fission harnessed in bombs. The potential was apocalyptic. Global war was no longer unthinkable.

A participant in the French Resistance, Beckett learned in 1943 that German troops were scouring Vaucluse villages near Avignon. In that area, very close, his Resistance pocket was hiding. Beckett's life was probably at stake. The playwright later stated that all his plays he considered valid were completed in the years 1945-1950, just after the period of his Resistance experiences.

Beckett began to compose Waiting for Godot in the Vaucluse, very likely aware that German troops might be nearing his hideout. His dramatic masterpiece, as Hugh Kenner and others have pointed out, almost surely was inspired by the life-or-death waiting Beckett endured during those existential hours. Time's normalcy was splintered, assassinated. Waiting for Godot theatricalized a total Proustian quest for time, for its substance.

As an entity, Beckett's drama exudes an exacerbated, uniquely French reaction. (Beckett's enduring Frenchness is certain, despite his Irish atavisms, phobias, and sources.) The germinal years for his plays, 1940-45, coincided roughly with his World War II experiences in France. Sartre, Camus, and other French writers of the Resistance had similar wellsprings of war inspirations during the period. Extraordinary stress, tension, the need for life-vs-death decisions involving oneself and others were unavoidable. At times, it seemed, so was new metaphysics.

Beckett's plays most often link Resistance tensions with those, peaceful but harassed, of 1945-1950. Waiting for Godot and Endgame indeterminately boil with the unresolved struggles incited by the Nazis, the Resistance, the Russian invasions of Eastern Europe, and the American nuclear menace.

It is true that Samuel Beckett did not design his plays for the instant. He is a visionary poet. He seeks to glimpse an infinite, the tangle of the universe, cosmic miasma devined through language and torn structure.

If Waiting for Godot and Endgame are ferocious and acid, especially when interpreted together, it is because Beckett, as he admitted, fought one implacable adversary: cosmic confusion.

Samuel Beckett's kaleidoscope of the post-atomic world as awesome muddle was in important ways analogous to that created by Friedrich Dürrenmatt, another outstanding savage comedy seer. The Swiss-German author of The Visit, more explosive in his dramas than Beckett, called the Cosmos a monster against which men have to fight. Dürrenmatt displays the consequences of this combat: "cosmic malaise."

Beckett's plays, more than "theater of the absurd," are constructed as wild, serpentine labyrinths. Enigmatic, they may crack open to show surprising metaphor and sense. In Waiting for Godot (1954, American version), Endgame (1958), and Krapp's Last Tape (1958), a dramatic being seeks through time on many levels a lost nether-self or some original alter ego, possibly a Dantesque guide. This mentor may have answers to the quester's ultimate puzzles—to those conundrums about the way the Cosmos functions in the medium of words and symbols. Belief-splintering, these enigmas ("Why must we keep reinterpreting the self in spatial time? Why is Time so excruciatingly hard to fill?) are the backbone of Beckett's metaphysical questioning.

On the whole, Beckett's plays will strike most audiences as dour and austere. How can they be comic, despite the devastated no-man's lands of Waiting for Godot and Endgame, the inward-bent anti-adventures of Krapp's Last Tape?

Do they mask derisory savagery? In a rare interview, the playwright helped to clarify this predicament. Beckett (he asserted) did not aim to darken twentieth-century muddles. He wanted to help bring about "renovation" by having a spectator focus sharply, without flinching, on the mess around him:

> "The confusion is not my invention...It is all around us and our only chance now is to let it in. The only

chance of renovation is to open our eyes and see the mess."[7]

Beckett's stance is simple. Anti-absurd and undogmatic, it defines the playwright's purpose, exposes his process. To combat dilemmas as they muddy and degrade the post-atomic era, we need to open wide all the mind's basements, all its windows. Ubiquitous confusion seeps in. We must breathe it in entirety. Only then, says Beckett, can understanding begin its new birth agonies.

Somber, curious viewpoints. Few theatergoers are prepared for them. Where, then are comic responses? Mixed, subtle, contradictory, they flout many of the contentions depended upon in farce before Beckett appeared. Theater's (or life's) petty networks of intricacies (a light that goes out, bodily malfunctions, Godot's "promise" unkept and the inscrutable compulsion of waiting, a branch that gives way to thwart a bum's suicide) are tiny curls, tangling, with no remedy thinkable.

These tangles, when artistically put into sharp relief and patterned as metaphor, can now and then arouse laughter. The clown's boot, a bad size, will not go on. It sticks. (Why the wrong size? And why does our Cosmos not seem to fit us? Why do we stick in its craw, as if we were something wrong-sized?) In uneasy identification with such a question, queasily, spectators laugh inside.

Samuel Beckett's comedies are thus serpentine and labyrinthine. There is no exit; they are mazes. They tantalize. Our sardonic humor reacts. In Godot, Endgame, Krapp's Last Tape, Happy Days (1961), Play (1964) and Beckett's less famous works for the stage, the self wanders, unknowing, through modern parables deprived of conclusions.

Beckett obviously has the genius of comic ferocity. Sometimes it devastates, as Germaine Brée has shown, when his dramatic uniqueness shears away non-essentials, creating fantastical and shattering humor:

81

> Beckett is...a contemporary Faust who, through the
> agency of his characters, indiscriminately, and with
> ferocious humor, undermines all our past and present
> attempts to give reality an intelligible structure, to
> "think out" our human situation...Beckett's verbal
> clowning produces...devastation, as do certain
> Jarry-like inventions which allow him to reduce our
> relations with the physical world to the status of a
> simple diagram...Beckett's fantasy and humor are...
> strangely mingled with ferocity and with compassion.[8]

It is true that Beckett's poetic fierceness carries a vast
current of the comic. Germaine Brée profoundly associates Beckett's "devastation" through his verbal originality with Jarry's
rarely understood semiotic inventions, each enabling us to see
the world as a simple diagram. Both savage-comic playwrights
mysteriously fuse ferocity and enigmatic, sub-stratum pity for
the human condition.

Beckett's outstanding plays, like his trilogy of novels,
intimate a dense, plodding progression. This advances irrevo-
cably inward. It traces an obsessive, ever-tightening trajec-
tory of the mind. Its path is almost, though not quite, concen-
tric. Each cycle is more taut than its predecessor. Incessant,
irregular whirlpools of memory and intellect, they bore deeper
and deeper toward Beckett's conjectural point of no return. That
point is ultimate mystery. It is the instant creativity runs out
forever. It is the last step on the precipice overlooking
nothingness.

For Beckett clearly hints reversion to some spiritual womb,
life's near-zero point. His plays spiral toward absence of
identity, toward a new species of gelid sterility and beauty,
once encased in Mallarmé's swan, seemingly trapped for eternity
in the symbolic ice.

Godot, the unfindable key to Beckett's theater, if we can
define him in any durable way, may embody a last iota of knowledge, a desperate gasp of human breath, if not a way one day to
free poetry's emprisoned swan.

Friedrich Dürrenmatt dramatizes other possibilities to face--
and sometimes to vanquish--near-zero points in a grinding Cosmos.
In his perplexing play, The Meteor (Der Meteor, 1966), the central figure, Wolfgang Schwitter, is an author and a Nobel Prize
winner who clamors to die but rejects life's end. Schwitter is
an undecipherable riddle for himself and for others.

To clarify angles of understanding for several of his most
baffling characters, including Schwitter, Dürrenmatt suggests
the term "verschlusselt" (interlocked, as in cryptography). In
this word, Dürrenmatt underlines something genuinely extraordinary. His "verschlusselt" characters are mixtures like conundrums, messages not yet decoded.

Concealed from all others, deep inside himself, Schwitter
is an enigma. A spectator guesses some sort of ferocious polyvalence. There are latent powers split, not quite operative.
One realizes that Schwitter's is a syndrome of semi-formless
corrosiveness, the very shape of savage comedy.

When largely construed, the same syndrome can be seen to
shape King Ubu's gruesome desires. In Albee's Who's Afraid of
Virginia Woolf?, parallel, though dissimilar, figurative conno-
tations are evident. Martha's loyalties are almost catastrophically deformed: undue respect for a prestigious father, patches
of love for a partially ineffectual husband, adoration of a son
not actually born, fascination by a youthful geneticist. None
really works. And Albee offers no sure ways to progress.

Eugene Ionesco (who migrated into theater from surrealist
poetry) implies other puzzles in fantasmagoria and a-logical
phantom-languages. In a Cosmos which would seem to be going
haywire, stampeding rhinoceroces are symptoms of Ionesco's terror
and bafflement. Human beings are smelting. They are transfig-
uring the essences of everyday contact and empathy. In Ionesco's
theater, a typical progression is argument (usually domestic)
expanding with irresistible power to bring closer the explosion

of the universe. For Ionesco, this metaphor is absolutely basic. Deformed intimacy leads to virulence and disintegration. Moral: after petty squabbles, the world itself may shatter. An eminently modern vision...Hydrogen bomb, arms proliferation? No doubt whatsoever; they are on Ionesco's mind. Though more obliquely than the Swiss-German satirist Dürrenmatt, Ionesco has forebodings of cosmic disaster, in the shattering of the earth's matter.

The first quandary, then, is the one which confronts the modern poet in the theater; how to express the most equivocal and perilous truths about men's interrelating in the atomic Cosmos without flames or estrangement.

In The Bald Soprano, a maid recites a wild poem obsessed with fire. Names and destinies rip. In the end, language catches fire and explodes. A different, somehow miniature universe begins: Smiths are now Martins; Martins are Smiths. Metamorphoses run amuk.

Dürrenmatt, in a remarkable interview of 1970, made crystal clear his view of his aims and preferences in theater:

> "Without art man is blind.
> Through the theater the dramatist tries to change the social reality of man...
> I write only comedies... (My method) is dialectical. I show the other side...
> Aristophanes I like. Shakespeare...
> I prefer tightly structured pieces. I also experiment with time..."[9]

As Violet Ketel noted, "The clash of war and peace is Dürrenmatt's theatrical obsession."[10] Why should this clash resound almost incessantly in the playwright's themes? The dramatist's logic is pointed; it is filled with horror of American military potential in the future:

> "The Swiss intellectual...is afraid of the American military and industrial world power, just as he is afraid of any world power...
> Peace is the problem, not war; war pushes the problems of peace aside, instead of solving them...
> To penetrate the basic human predicament is more

important than to fly to the moon, which is nothing but an escape from the earth and thereby an escape from Man."[11]

TEN: SAVAGE COMEDY'S MOST DEEPLY-ROOTED OSBESSIONS

What makes these comedies "savage"? A group of deeply-rooted obsessions seems to be imbedded in them, almost ineradicable. They can be outlined in schematic form:

(1) Dread metamorphoses forewarn the spectator of dehumanization, even death.

(2) One consequence is a neo-Hamletic _Angst_, coloring shadowy comedy with wry, hidden ironies.

(3) Queasy, held-in laughter is a main sensation.

(4) Above all is the notion that the Cosmos has somehow been wrenched out of its orbit; it refuses to run smoothly.

(5) In riposte, savage comedies engage in battle against a grinding Cosmos and the wars it ignites.

(6) Prefiguration of deathly ruthlessness. It reverberates Rimbaud's prophecy, "The time of assassins..." and Yeats' "After us the savage King," as it foreshadows Hitler, Stalin, and pogroms everywhere.

(7) Death is a primary _comic_ antagonist.

(8) Comedy, in derisive dread of death, nearly supplants tragedy.

(9) Life is felt as miasma or reversing whirlpool.

(10) Nightmare, seen in metaphor, is a frequent type of plot.

(11) Straight-line plot breaks. It is replaced by fragments or overlappings.

(12) Death's apparent animality brings counterattack, at times nether-human.

Jarry's _King Ubu_ is the fountainhead of modern savage comedy in Western theater. In germ, it contains what is coming on many experimental stages, in the United States as in Europe. Dürrenmatt's _The Physicists_ and _The Visit_ are fruitions, full of foreboding, modern sound and anti-exploitative fury. Arrabal's most

extravagant, cannibalistic play (The Architect and the Emperor
of Assyria) and Albee's rapacious and shredding comedy, Who's
Afraid of Virginia Woolf? are summaries of savage modes. Each
clarifies avenues to outlandishy new esthetics.

Jarry's King Ubu is virtually a charade, impelled by obsessions. Some are couched in mists of oblique metaphor and ultra-
fantastic hyperboles. King Ubu's sepulchral conscience is one
way, one key. A semiotic clue comes when Ubu and fellow con-
spirators, in combat in Poland (explained as "nowhere" by Jarry),
are attacked by a huge bear. Alone, Ubu cravenly flees from
the monster. His cohorts slay it. Reappearing, safe, Ubu joins
in a feast on the carcass.

Assassin, usurper-King, Ubu announces in stentorian style:
"Combat of the voracious against the rugged tenacious." Ubu's
universal-war metaphor is potent, though overdone. All existence is seen as rapacious war. This is one of Jarry's most
anthropomorphic and gloomy images of life as ravenous battle,
on paths toward extermination of the human species.

Jarry's primal clusters of metaphors join political murders
and wars of several kinds. King Ubu's mock combats tell us hyper-
bolically of the erosions of inner fighting. This is Jarry's
main theme in his drama. It is unremitting rapaciousness, eating
away the core of the individual. An obsessive personal vision
looms. King Ubu's universal ravages hint that voracity swallows
up human consciences, minds, and bodies.

Ubu spins brutal daydreams of "debraining" Mother Ubu and
stripping her spinal cord. Sequel plays repeat this obsession.
Farcical, macabre, the wild daydream is both metaphor and omen
in its excruciating foresight of truths to come.

A few decades after Ubu's daydreams of torture, surgeon's
scalpels performed lobotomies, removed major parts of nervous
systems, inserted artificial organs. "The voracious" had become
methodical and real. Ubu's simple disappearing and death machine,
"the trap," which tossed away unwanted adversaries, is a miniature

invention for mass-destruction. History has not been short-sighted in inventing such deathly contrivances, from Hitler's gas chambers to nerve gas in every "up-to-date" nation, lasers, and atomic fission bombs.

In King Ubu, surfaces of ribald glee mask terror. Many savage comedies from 1896 to 1970 rephrase this captivity in a kind of dream-like dread. At times (as in Beckett's and Dürrenmatt's most shattering plays), it implies metaphysical Angst and fear. Beckett's combined love-dread of an unknown void, Genet's turned-topsy-turvy universe (The Balcony), Albee's screams of withering humor as vulnerable shield for the psyche's shudders, Dürrenmatt's moral and bodily resurrections are a provocative group of examples.

King Ubu's crescendos of near-animality cry out in trepidation, not in bravery. His conscience, echoing in a devoured bear, does not flee. He has gobbled an animal-like dread, or thinks he has. Without clear purpose or warning, Ubu figuratively foresees an era when scientists and doctors, perhaps like omniscient carnivore-bears, will slash willy-nilly. Thus what looked grotesque in 1896 turned to reality. (Dürrenmatt's The Physicists, some forty years later, accurately showed the danger of hydrogen bombs, or even worse.)

Dürrenmatt, who is the son of a pastor, is one of modern theater's most catastrophic cosmic seers. His Furies are war profiteers, menacing science and technology, crass nationalisms. The Swiss-German playwright builds shudder and shock more candid than Jarry's and Ionesco's. He twists metaphysical secrets: the keys to the Cosmos. Dürrenmatt's masterpiece may be The Visit. Does it fit the usual aims of comedy, even of dark comedy? Rarely. A ruthless heroine, Claire, manipulates dirty luchre. She devastates her former lover's inner fiber and that of his village. Mercilessly caricatured, little people's avidity is the target of her derision, her total scorn. Feminine rule is on the rise. This is one of Dürrenmatt's most striking forecasts.

Dürrenmatt perhaps saw further than other playwrights into the turmoil of atomic fission and outer space, the very orbits of unknown planets. But a number of savage-comic authors were surprising seers. Jarry saw a weird no-man's land almost devoid of visible war; he foresaw cruel sciences and medicine. In large part, they have now materialized. Apollinaire presaged the serious ups-and-downs of national birthrates, as well as hermaphroditic sexes, in joke or not. Surrealists, Roger Vitrac most violently, saw the passage of wars into wars, of warfare generations into warfare generations and the resultant collapsing of hopes. Picasso played with anthropomorphism, as Arrabal and several other playwrights would later, somewhat more literally. Arrabal even speculated about transvestism, sex switches, and outright cannibalism.

Without sacrificing repressed and black laughter, Salacrou and Anouilh had written prolifically of the heart's suppressions, its attempts to break loose from binding chains. On occasion these breakthroughs did occur, with frank derision, sometimes even a rare, semi-happy ending. Savage comedy was not all forbidding or gray. But by and large, stormy grayness, if not tempest, prevailed. Cocteau, on the margins of both surrealism and savage comedy, offered exceptions: especially Wedding on the Eiffel Tower, a light-hearted romp. Apollinaire's The Breasts of Tiresias is another zany example. Several surrealist plays are also frivolous, rather than somber or bellicose.

Chaos and near-chaos hide in language. Languages, as they burst to bits in The Bald Soprano and The Lesson, by Ionesco, are illustrative. Language almost turns into character, as it does in the maid's famous poem on fire in The Bald Soprano. At last it happens. Smiths, after their fiery explosion in words, when words lose definable meaning, are transmuted into Martins. Words become other words; persons who utter them become other persons. And the play goes on, a cycle of gibberish which has gathered new meanings, cyclical overturnings.

In plays by Dürrenmatt, Jarry, Ionesco, Albee, Mrozek (Tango, 1965), Pinter, and others, new scathing-comic myth takes outline. A new Prometheus, a new Icarus come to the fore, demanding knowledge of Cosmic principles and fires. Cosmic promises along with its perils. A spectator needs sharpened optics as he peers into savage comedy's ever-growing multiplicity of universes. For, as Ionesco has reminded us, the poet's first task is to "impose his universe," to make us see it as it looks to him.

The natal womb seems to be Samuel Beckett's only ultimate haven, his return. His Godot hardly strikes chords from this earth. Perhaps a different one? The famous "waiting" may be in expectation of another Cosmos, or maybe not. There is no certain way of telling. Nor can we be sure where Endgame is. On this earth? Possibly. But just as likely, elsewhere. This is Beckett's intellectual ferocity, in his unworldly scenes when life on this earth appears more postulate than certainty. If Ionesco's plot cycles turn outward, covering each other, Beckett's go forever inward, toward guts and spleen. A final, resting womb is not far away.

American history, strangely enough, is Edward Albee's primordial theme. He never deviates too distantly from it. In Who's Afraid of Virginia Woolf?, George and Martha are clear heirs of the Washingtons. George, a historian, is on occasion timorous and befuddled, as was American history at the time of the Viet-Nam war. Martha, a sort of lost earth-mother, is not sure from where her next sources of power and strength are to come. Genetics tempts her. In Albee's plot, this is an error. Nick, the young scientist who takes Martha to bed, is spurious. He has no lasting power. He is a dud.

The humanists' fabricated "son" suggests little more hope, even though he is for the moment false. He at least leads them toward possible directions, toward some potential in new humanistic conjectures. Like Beckett, Anouilh, Mrozek, Dürrenmatt, and possibly Pinter, Ionesco and Albee are not without a new

90

kind of hope. But their hopes lie couched, most often, in enigma, conundrum. Aspiration is findable in radical shiftings of theatrical devices: stage tonalities, rhythms, signposts for waiting and final knowing. As in Beckett's meandering or semi-frozen plays, an immense patience is called for, and quite often exacted from the spectator, who is virtually lost. In part, savage comedy's apparent "straying" is an attempted flight from the ancient minotaur's maze, the maze hiding new knowledge itself. Where to find the labyrinthine exit is a secret.

Compulsion, obsession and dreamlike dread are the hallmarks of savage comedy. To be sure, some scenes are less gruesome or fearful than others. Yet the mode's bizarre structures take impetus from these drives, more than from any others. Inside such dire instincts, neither confidence of usual sorts nor bright optimism belong. A product of wars, terrors, and dour expectations (World Wars I and II, Viet-Nam, uncontrolled inflation in many countries), savage theater is unquestionably an amalgam of its own times. Prophecy, as in Dürrenmatt's The Physicists, may be anticipatory of the atomic worst. As sheer metaphor of what happens when new scientific knowledge looms, this drama, a prototype, is a brilliant hint of peril. It has led the way for savage comedies in Western nations. This is perhaps the mode's most far-reaching scope.

Why then "comedy"? Tragedy has virtually disappeared since about 1900. A void was left. Some of the darkest of wild comedies seem destined to fill the gap. Killing, since King Ubu and some surrealist theater, has been a comic leit-motif. So, on occasion, has been hate, even murder. Savage comedy is a widespread form of revolt. It leaves little room for the old, debonair, laughable pretenses, even for the frivolous surfaces, of the purported "Belle Epoque" which preceded it.

Notes

1. SAVAGE COMEDY: JARRY'S KING UBU TO DURRENMATT AND ALBEE

   1. W.B. Yeats, The Autobiographies of W.B. Yeats (Garden City, N.Y.: Doubleday, 1958), p. 234.

   2. Michael Benedikt and George Wellwarth, Modern French Theatre (N.Y.: Dutton, 1966), xi.

   3. W.B. Yeats, ibid.

   4. Cf. The Irish Times (Dublin), Feb. 26, 1975.

2. A QUEASY COSMOS

3. RIPOSTE

4. SCIENCE AND IMAGINATION CROSSED: SAVAGE COMEDY AND ITS TRANSGRESSIONS OF RATIONAL FRONTIERS

   1. Violet Ketel, interview with Friedrich Dürrenmatt, Journal of Modern Literature, vol. I, no. 1 (1970), p. 88.

5. WHIMSY WITH SAVAGE UNDERTONES: APOLLINAIRE, PICASSO

   1. Guillaume Apollinaire, Oeuvres Poétiques (Paris: Gallimard, Bibliothèque de la Pléiade), p. 22.

   2. F. Dürrenmatt and V. Ketel, interview, Journal of World Literature, vol. I, no. 1 (1970), p. 88.

6. SURREALISM'S SAVAGERY ON STAGE

   1. Ionesco, Préface, The Painting (in Benedikt and Wellwarth, Modern French Theatre, p. 360).

   2. T. Tzara, The Gas Heart, in ibid., p. 132.

   3. Ibid., p. 137.

7. FIERCE DISSOLVENTS

8. DREAD TURNS COMIC: A NEW GENERATION

9. THE COUSINS OF THE ABSURD

    1. Robert Hatch, "Laugh Now, Pay Later," _Horizon_, March 1963, pp. 106-07.

10. MASTERWORKS

    1. E. Ionesco, "Mes pièces et moi," _Notes et Contre-Notes_ (Paris: Gallimard, 1954).

    2. E. Ionesco, _Na_ (Paris, 1934).

    3. E. Ionesco, _Entretiens avec Claude Bonnefoy_ (Paris: Belfond, 1966), p. 91.

    4. Kenneth Tynan, "Something for Everybody," _The Observer_ (London), April 28, 1957.

    5. Fernando Arrabal, dust jacket, _Théâtre panique_ (Paris: Bourgois, 1967).

    6. Martin Esslin, _The Theater of the Absurd_ (Garden City, N.Y.: Doubleday, 1969), p. 222.

    7. S. Beckett, interview with Tom Driver, "Beckett by the Madeleine," _Columbia University Forum_, 4 (Summer, 1961), p. 22.

    8. Germaine Brée, "The Strange World of Beckett's 'grands articulés,' in M.J. Friedman, ed., _Samuel Beckett Now_ (Chicago, University of Chicago Press, 1970), pp. 74-75.

    9. F. Dürrenmatt, interview with Violet Ketel, _Journal of Modern Literature_, vol. I, no. 1 (1970), pp. 92-93.

    10. Violet Ketel, _ibid._, p. 89.

    11. F. Dürrenmatt, _ibid._, p. 89.

11. SAVAGE COMEDY'S MOST DEEPLY ROOTED OBSESSIONS

12. POSTFACE